The Metadata Handbook

Second Edition

The Metadata Handbook

A Book Publisher's Guide to Creating and Distributing Metadata for Print and Ebooks

Renée Register & Thad McIlroy

Second Edition

Columbus, Ohio
2015

The Metadata Handbook
Second Edition

*A Book Publisher's Guide to Creating and
Distributing Metadata for Print and Ebooks*

www.themetadatahandbook.com

Published by DATACURATE, LLC

379 Tibet Road
Columbus, OH 43202-1419
United States of America
www.datacurate.com

Copyright ©2015 by Renée Register and Thad McIlroy

All rights reserved.

This book or parts thereof may not be reproduced in any form, stored in a retrieval system, or transmitted in any form by any means — electronic, mechanical, photocopy, recording or otherwise — without prior written permission of the publisher, except as provided by United States of America copyright law. All logos and trademarks are the property of the respective trademark owners. ® and ™ denote registered trademarks in the U.S. and other countries.

ISBN: 978-0-9858288-6-8

Bulk purchases and site licenses are available at a significant discount from retail. Please contact the publisher for details.

Cover design, book design, and graphics by Adam Rowe
www.admrwe.com

Table of Contents

Introduction x

Part 1:
Book Industry Players and the Metadata Lifecycle

Part 1 explores the path and evolution of metadata through publishing and bookselling activities and channels and describes the players that create, distribute, enhance, and use metadata.

CHAPTER 1 1
The Metadata Lifecycle

CHAPTER 2 5
The Players

- Publishers
- Book Data Aggregators
- Wholesalers, Distributors, and Ebook Aggregators
- Retailers
- Libraries
- Metadata Management Vendors

Part 2:
Book Industry Metadata Standards

Part 2 outlines the history and development of book identifiers and book metadata standards, the organizations that administer the standards, and the role of standards in facilitating efficient data exchange in support of e-commerce.

CHAPTER 3 .... **18**
A Brief History of Metadata Standards and Practices

CHAPTER 4 .... **23**
Book Industry Standards for Sharing Metadata

- ISBN and Other Identifiers
  - ISBN, ISNI, ISTC, SAN, LCCN
- Metadata Schemes
  - ONIX for Books
  - Other Schemes
- Standards for Subjects
  - Book Industry Standards
  - Library Standards

CHAPTER 5 .... **37**
National and International Standards Organizations

- ISO and NISO
- The International ISBN Agency and National ISBN Registry Agencies
- EDItEUR and the ONIX Standard

Part 3:
Essential Metadata Elements

Part 3 describes types of book metadata and the essential information about a book needed to fully support description, discovery, selection, and commerce needs. This section also explores the ways in which various metadata elements are used behind the scenes to drive search engines and machine-based decisions on what books to display to which readers.

CHAPTER 6 43
Essential Elements for All Books

CHAPTER 7 49
Enhancing Metadata to Stand Out in the Marketplace

CHAPTER 8 51
Search Engine Optimization, Keywords, and Subjects

- SEO and Keywords
- Keywords and BISAC Subject Headings
- Bookseller Website Search Engines
- General Search Engines

CHAPTER 9 54
Optimizing Product Metadata for Digital Publishing

- The Essential Elements
- Ebooks and ISBNs
- Expanded Options for Digital Content in ONIX 3.0

CHAPTER 10 56
Metadata in Digital Content Files

- Uses of Metadata in Digital Content Files
- Metadata in the EPUB File Format
- Metadata in Proprietary Digital Formats

CHAPTER 11 59
Metadata for Self-Publishers and Small Publishers

- Identifiers: ISBN, Proprietary Identifier Systems, and Industry Databases
- Product Metadata Options in Self-Publishing Services
- Digital File Metadata Options in Self-Publishing Services
- Ebook Distribution Options in Self-Publishing Services

Part 4:
Metadata Best Practices and Certification Programs

Part 4 discusses certification and accreditation programs administered by national publishing industry organizations. These programs evaluate and rate publisher metadata for compliance with industry standards, recommended core elements, and best practices.

CHAPTER 12 .... **63**

What Are Metadata Best Practices and How Are They Identified?

- Best Practices and Industry Standards
- The Role of Industry Organizations in Defining Best Practices

CHAPTER 13 .... **65**

BISG's Best Practices for Product Metadata: Guide for North American Data Senders and Receivers

- History of BISG Best Practices Documentation
- Intended Audience
- Structure and Format of *Best Practices of Product Metadata*
- A Closer Look at Best Practices for One Metadata Element
- Integrating Best Practices into Organizational Workflows

CHAPTER 14 .... **75**

Metadata Certification Programs

- What is Certification?
- The BISG Product Certification Program (PDCP)
- The Evaluation Process
- Fields Reviewed by the PDCP Certification Panel
- Product Data Certification in Other Countries
- Levels of Certification

Part 5:
Metadata and the Future of Publishing

Part 5 discusses how metadata standards and practices are evolving in response to the increased importance of digital publishing, the rise of self-publishing, shifts in the roles of publishing industry players, and changes in reader expectations. In conclusion, the authors share their thoughts on the meaning of these trends for the future of publishing and the role of metadata.

CHAPTER 15 .... **79**
Trends in Book Publishing and Metadata

CHAPTER 16 .... **91**
Thoughts on the Future of Publishing and Metadata

Glossary 96

Bibliography & References 109

Industry Organizations 115

Vendor Directory 121

About the Authors 128

Introduction

*The Metadata Handbook is for book publishers, including self-publishers and small publishers, who wish to optimize the dissemination of complete, compelling, and accurate information about their books throughout the publishing supply chain. This **Handbook** describes the metadata that accompanies each new book through the many activities necessary to propel it into the marketplace, to support discovery, and to increase sales potential.*

The ability to describe products completely and accurately and to efficiently share that data with trading partners and consumers is essential for e-commerce in every industry. In this respect book metadata is unexceptional. But every product and every industry has unique aspects that its product metadata attempts to reflect.

It's possible to sell a book online with just a few pieces of information, such as ISBN, title, and price. But providing minimal metadata limits opportunities for a book to be discovered, create a buzz, or make a sale. Success in the virtual marketplace requires the distribution of book metadata that fully supports findability and discovery, provides information that engages the potential reader, and contains all the information needed to support business transactions and business intelligence. Metadata must also meet the needs of booksellers and other trading partners. Many major receivers of publisher metadata require that certain metadata elements are present and correctly formatted and may reject metadata that fails to meet standards, resulting in lost sales.

For digital books, metadata entirely takes the place of all the physical organization, display, and browsing opportunities possible in bricks-and-mortar stores. For readers who prefer to buy books online, this is true for physical books as well.

Metadata that is thoughtfully created and shared using industry standards and best practices supports all aspects of publishing and bookselling. And when creating, controlling, and monitoring book metadata is fully integrated into each publication stage, the result is a powerful asset for effective selling across traditional and evolving sales channels as well as for the collection and analysis of sales results and market trends.

With the growth of digital content and publishing platforms, selling options have expanded from the traditional wholesalers and retailers to include sellers specializing in ebooks and easier options for selling directly from author or publisher websites. Digital formats are also more closely tied to their respective distribution channels (Amazon's proprietary KF8 format for Kindle, EPUB for Nook, etc.) than traditional hardcover, trade, and mass-market paperback formats ever were, so it's crucial that metadata enable users to select a format compatible with their reading device. To maximize discovery and sales potential, metadata should be complete, correctly formatted, and consistent for all formats and across all sales channels.

While metadata is a science of great breadth and is relevant to many industries and endeavors, this book focuses specifically on metadata used to describe, market, and sell books throughout the publishing supply chain. Rather than a how-to book, the *Handbook* is intended to be an industry reference. The reader can turn to it as the authoritative source on best practices in the day-to-day use of metadata in book publishing. The central goal of the *Handbook* is to describe and provide references to information about book metadata standards and best practices that are presently endorsed in the United States, the United Kingdom, and Canada.

The authors bring significant experience in U.S. and Canadian publishing-related activities but do not claim first-hand experience within the UK market. We have relied in part on the resources issued by major publishing industry organizations in each of the three countries.

The *Handbook* does not specifically cover any of the other countries or regions that publish English-language books, including Australia, South Africa, The Republic of Ireland, India, or any other country where English is not the first language. We are interested in hearing from parties who would like to adapt the information in this book for their home market(s).

The Metadata Handbook does not duplicate readily available documentation but presents an overview of metadata's role in the publisher supply chain. It collects and consolidates information about industry guidelines and resources into one volume for use as a reference in the practice of book data management.

New in This Edition

This edition is fully updated and expanded to include the most recent information on metadata standards, practices, and use in the publishing industry.

Part 1, *Book Industry Players and the Metadata Lifecycle* is revised.

Part 2, *Book Industry Metadata Standards* is revised throughout for consistency with the latest versions of industry standards and best practices documentation.

The *Identifiers* section of Part 2, Chapter 4, *Book Industry Standards for Sharing Metadata*, includes expanded and updated information on International Standard Name Identifier (ISNI) and International Standard Text Code (ISTC).

A new section on *Metadata Schemes* is added to Chapter 4. Information on ONIX is incorporated into this section and it also includes new subsections covering *Dublin Core* and *scema.org*.

A new section on *Standards for Subjects* was added and includes information on Thema as well as information about BISAC, BIC, and library standards.

Part 3, *Essential Metadata Elements*, is revised throughout for consistency with industry recommendations included in latest edition of Book Industry Study Group (BISG) best practices documentation, *Best Practices for Product Metadata: Guide for North American Senders and Receivers*, published in 2014.

Three new chapters are added to Part 3.
- A new chapter on *Search Engine Optimization, Keywords, and Subjects* (Chapter 8)
- A new chapter called *Metadata in Digital Content Files* outlines options for metadata embedded within digital content files (Chapter 10)
- A new chapter specifically addressing *Metadata for Self-Publishers and Small Publishers* (Chapter 11)

Part 4, *Metadata Best Practices and Industry Certification Programs*, is fully revised to provide an overview and guide to using *Best Practices for Product Metadata: Guide for North American Senders and Receivers*, published in 2014 by the Book Industry Study Group (BISG) in coordination with BookNet Canada.

Part 5, *Metadata and the Future of Publishing*, includes updates from industry experts on trends in metadata and publishing.

The **Bibliography and References** section is revised and expanded to include recent publications and revisions of existing documentation.

New entries are added to the **Glossary** and some entries are revised to reflect the most recent information.

Part 1
Book Industry Players and the Metadata Lifecycle

In Part 1, we outline the role and lifecycle of metadata in major publishing activities and sales channels. "Players" covered include:

- Publishers, including trade, professional, educational, independent, and self-publishers
- Book metadata aggregators, such as Bowker and Nielsen
- Retailers, including independent booksellers, chain bookstores, and online retailers
- Digital-only ebook aggregators such as OverDrive and ebrary
- Library metadata aggregators and library metadata uses
- Vendors specializing in products and services supporting book metadata management and distribution activities

We discuss how and why metadata changes as it flows through the publishing process and then through various reseller systems, platforms, and websites.

Part 2
Book Industry Metadata Standards

Part 2 covers existing and emerging standards important for bookselling in the 21st century. It offers a brief history of metadata standards and practices, introduces standards commonly used within the publishing industry, and discusses the national and international organizations and registries that administer and support them.

As with most major industries, data standards evolved to support the consistent flow of information in electronic form across the supply chain. The need for identifiers and data transmission standards became acute as computer technology became an important part of trade. Early numbering systems in the 1960s grew into the first International Standard Book Number (ISBN) system; the need for machine-to-machine transmission of business data between trading partners led to the development of Electronic Data Interchange (EDI) standards; and the explosive growth of the internet and online retailing required XML-based communication of robust book metadata, resulting in the development of ONIX (Online Information Exchange) for Books as the international standard for sharing book industry product information.

Part 3
Essential Metadata Elements

The ONIX for Books Product Information Message defines and supports hundreds of data fields carrying information about a publication. Publishers are not required to use all the fields, and not all the fields are applicable to every book. Part 3 lists and describes metadata elements considered essential for bookselling and explains why they're important.

Some of the ways metadata elements function in an online selling environment are not immediately apparent by viewing a title record display on a website. Part 3 explores how these essential elements are used behind the scenes in addition to their more obvious use in direct title search.

Part 3 also includes chapters providing information specific to digital publishing and information about metadata for self-publishers and small publishers.

Part 4
Metadata Best Practices and Certification Programs

Part 4 includes an overview of industry-recommended metadata elements, guidelines for applying these elements, and rules for using the ONIX standard. The *Handbook* collects basic information about the organizations and their recommended best practices into one reference work.

Book industry organizations administer programs designed to help publishers ensure compliance with industry standards and practices. Part 4 describes how these programs work and why publishers may wish to seek accreditation.

Part 5
Metadata and the Future of Publishing

In Part 5, we conclude with observations from industry leaders on the importance of metadata and how metadata standards and practices continue to evolve along with the rapidly changing nature of publishing itself.

The authors hope *The Metadata Handbook* will serve as an essential reference for publishers. Ultimately, the goal of this *Handbook* is to help connect readers to books by explaining how to best use metadata as an essential part of this endeavor.

Part 1: Book Industry Players and the Metadata Lifecycle

Chapter 1: The Metadata Lifecycle

Metadata goes along for the ride throughout the life of a book. Title data is created and maintained internally for production tracking purposes and enters the marketplace when the publisher is ready initiate the process of announcing a forthcoming publication, marketing the book, and accepting pre- and post-publication orders. Metadata use continues throughout the life of the title and plays a role any time the book is sold, even as a used copy.

Metadata should accurately express all known information about a book as it enters the marketplace. It should be updated with important changes or additions to title information prior to the official publication or on-sale date, and should receive further updates to reflect important events or activities relating to the book after publication.

Some metadata may be attached to a book even before an author completes the work. There is usually a working title, information about the contributor(s), a general idea of the genre or subject matter of the title, and a projected publication date.

For traditional publishers this early metadata is recorded and stored as soon as a decision is made to acquire or develop a new book. Self-publishers have basic metadata once a commitment to publish is made. Larger publishers use content management and production systems to capture metadata. Smaller publishers generally use a homegrown database or Excel-style spreadsheet.

This preliminary data must be shared externally for ISBN registration and so actually enters the marketplace at that point. However, the timing for officially sharing metadata through direct feeds to resellers, and/or to potential readers through a publisher website, varies based on the publisher's marketing strategy and expected publication date. In most cases, traditional publishing houses expose select information to major marketing channels at least six months prior to the publication date.

Listed below are the major publishing activities that are accompanied by supporting metadata. In an ideal world, the same record grows to support every relevant publishing activity rather than being re-created and stored multiple times in multiple places across organizations.

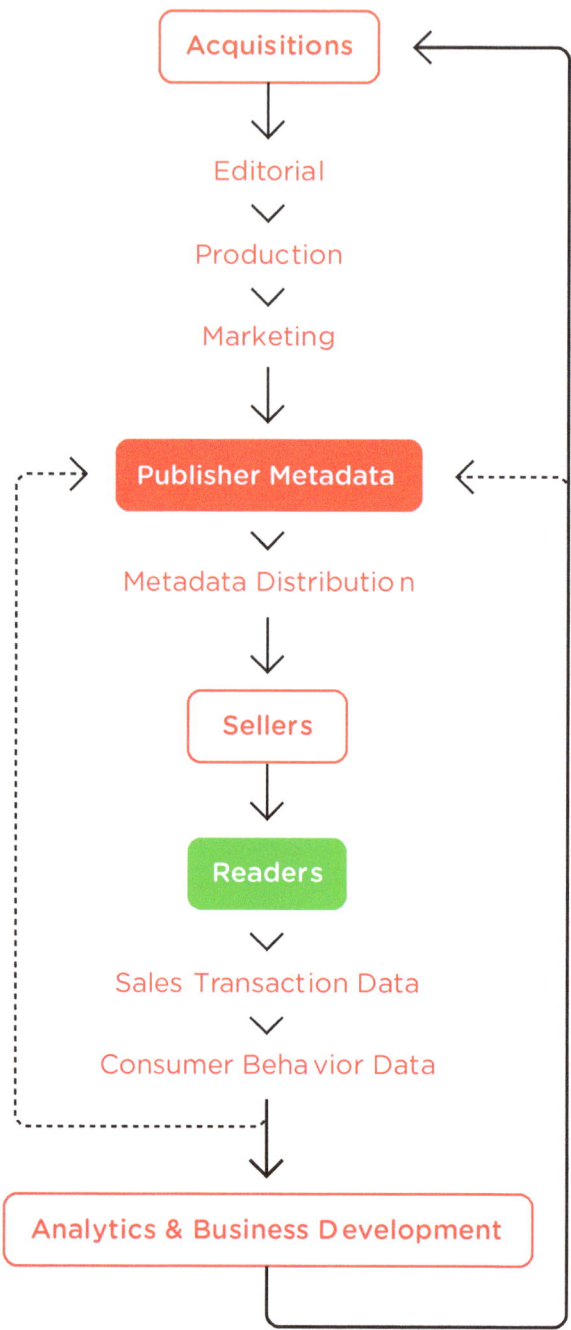

- Acquisitions
  - Content acquisition
    · Initial title metadata
    · Metadata for ISBN registration
- Editorial
  - Metadata about content and contributors
- Production
  - Metadata about size and format
- Marketing
  - Prepublication marketing
  - Publication date marketing
  - Post-publication marketing
- Metadata Distribution
  - Prepublication metadata
  - Prepublication metadata changes and additions
  - Post-publication metadata changes and additions
- Sellers and Readers
  - Sales Transaction Data
    · Prepublication sales transactions
    · Post-publication sales transactions
  - Consumer Behavior Data
    · User search and discovery
    · User feedback and ratings
- Analytics and Business Intelligence

Metadata grows and evolves throughout the stages of publication and across the life of the book. Many players create, distribute, enhance, and use book metadata, and this data may be changed many times through multiple channels. Sometimes changes are pushed from publishers to trading partners as information about the book evolves or changes. Examples include pre-publication title changes, the addition of the cover image once it's available, and providing information about final pagination once this is determined in the production process. Trading partners also adapt metadata for quality and usability within their internal systems and discovery platforms.

The industry often refers to "upstream" and "downstream" metadata. Upstream metadata is information created near the beginning of the publishing cycle. It originates with the publisher or content creator and then flows downstream to supply-chain resellers, trading partners, and ultimately to the reader. Most publishers, including self-publishers, sell books through multiple channels and so must push data downstream to multiple partners. Even if books are sold directly from a publisher website, most publishers also establish relationships with preferred selling partners to maximize opportunities to reach readers.

These downstream partners ingest the data for use in their own systems in support of their business needs and for use in their proprietary products and services. Reseller products and services include ordering platforms and websites for customer selection and purchase, title databases and data feeds, and especially in the wholesale environment, complex profile-driven recommendation and approval services for business-to-business customers such as retailers and libraries.

Data aggregators, wholesalers, and retail partners handle a much higher volume of data than individual publishers and have systemic checks in place for data quality and validity. Most also maintain professional staff devoted to metadata.

The diagram on the next page illustrates metadata flow between the major industry players. In Chapter 2, we will look at each of these channels and the role each plays in the metadata lifecycle.

Metadata Life Cycle

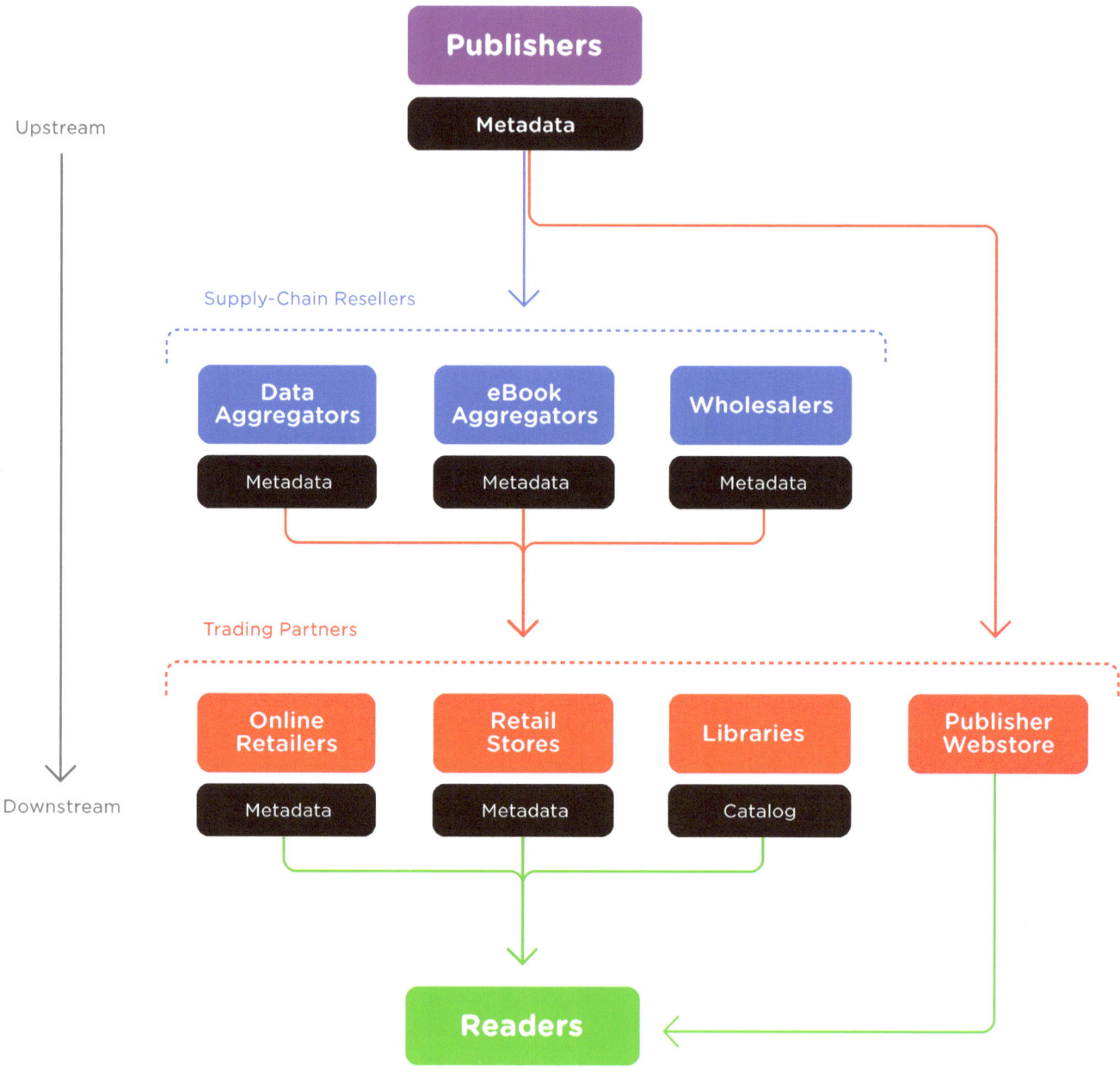

Chapter 2: **The Players**

Table of Contents

Publishers 6

· Trade Publishers 7
· Professional and Scholarly Publishers 7
· Educational Publishers 8
· Small and Independent Publishers 8
· Self-Publishers 9
· Digital Publishing 10

Book Data Aggregators 11

Wholesalers, Distributors, and
Ebook Aggregators 12

Retailers 14

· Independent Bookstores 14
· Chain Bookstores 15
· Online Retailers 15

Libraries 16

Metadata Management Vendors 17

The number and types of players in the marketplace (including new vendors in the digital publishing space) and the complexity of the publisher supply chain continue to grow. This results in additional challenges for publishers in the creation and distribution of books and their accompanying metadata. In 2012, the Book Industry Study Group sponsored a study conducted by Magellan Media Consulting to "map the flow of metadata across the publishing supply chain." The resulting publication, *The Development, Use, and Modification of Book Product Metadata*, was released in 2012.

The study emphasizes the existence of multiple metadata feeds, touch points, and modifications throughout the product and metadata lifecycle. Modifications to metadata aren't always shared among all the players, in part because of the specific metadata uses, needs, and proprietary systems of different types of resellers, but also because of the increasing volume of metadata and the number of data streams now required for distribution among all the players.

This chapter gives an overview of major players in the publisher supply chain, the contributions each makes to the metadata lifecycle, and the various ways metadata is used to support the business needs of the players.

Publishers

Formal metadata creation begins with the publisher. Publishers, including self-publishers, are responsible for the final product readers will see in the marketplace. They are also responsible for creating and packaging the information about the book (metadata) that is distributed to selling partners and used for marketing, merchandising, buying, and selling.

The process starts internally as the publisher decides a book will be published, acquires rights to publish a book (if the author is not also the publisher), collects and stores basic information about the book (such as author, working title, and general subject or genre), and obtains an ISBN. Basic information about the book is part of the ISBN assignment process and is often submitted at least six months in advance of the expected publication date.

The initial metadata is used to track a book through editorial and production processes, to prepare marketing materials, and to provide information to selling partners (retailers, wholesalers, etc.). Most major wholesalers, retailers, and distributors want this information six months in advance of publication if possible.

Book data is submitted electronically to supply chain trading partners described in the following sections. They have requirements for how book data is submitted and usually require certain information to be present in the record before accepting it into their systems. In addition to basic fields describing the book (title, author, etc.), information about the binding and/or digital format(s) of the book must be provided along with information needed to sell the book (price, discount, and territorial rights, for example.)

Publishers must be able to package and export book data in an acceptable form for transmission. The international standard for sharing book data in electronic form is the ONIX for Books Product Information Format. Essential data elements and best practices for creating, packaging, and transmitting metadata to trading partners are described in subsequent chapters.

Some publishers do transmit metadata in Excel spreadsheets, but there are now services and tools available to convert book data stored in other formats to the ONIX standard. Vendors providing help with ONIX are covered in the **Metadata Management Vendors** section of this chapter.

Small publishers and self-publishers with a single title (or very few titles) may need to submit metadata by completing online forms provided by sellers. It's still important to make sure data submitted title-by-title is as complete and accurate as possible.

As a book moves through the production process, additional information becomes available. The title might change, pricing could be adjusted, the number of pages is determined, a table of contents might be added, a cover image is created, and a description is written. New data and updates must be distributed to the trading partners in the same manner as the original data. There is a general expectation that the data for a product should be essentially complete and correct at least four months prior to publication.

This information is important for bookselling activities, including the reader's discovery and selection experience, and should be shared with trading partners as it becomes available. Attending to the evolution and lifecycle of book data can create challenges. Publishers (metadata senders) must have a way to identify and extract information that is added after the initial data transmission or resubmit the entire record on a periodic basis. Trading partners (metadata receivers) must have a way to replace and add information to the existing record.

The need to create, maintain, and distribute metadata is common among all publishers because it is an essential part of bookselling today. But there are many types of publishers, and the challenges differ based on size, target markets, sales channels, and other factors. Covering all of these factors and challenges would require much more than a chapter, but the following sections offer an overview of major publishing categories. In the **Industry Organizations** section of the *Handbook* you will find information about organizations that provide information and support for publishers in general and about organizations serving specific types of publishers.

Trade Publishers

Trade publications are marketed to the general consumer, and trade publishers are responsible for more than half of the books published in the English language. In the United States, trade publishing also accounts for about 50 percent of net sales. Trade books are aimed at the largest possible audience and seek the widest possible distribution through major wholesalers, retailers, and libraries.

Challenges

Trade publishers create, maintain, and distribute metadata for many titles and have relationships with most supply chain players. Most have multiple imprints with their own identities, marketing strategies, and metadata variations. Imprints can be business units of publishing houses but are essentially "brands." The books published under an imprint may have a defining genre, subject, or character, such as mystery fiction, literary fiction, or business books. The imprint could be aimed at a particular audience, such as children or young adults.

There may even be several publishing groups within the umbrella of a larger publishing corporation that are then further subdivided into imprints. For example, Hachette Book Group includes the publishing groups Grand Central Publishing, Little, Brown and Company, and Faith Books, among others. Under each publishing group (each with its own identity) there are further imprints. Imprints under Grand Central Publishing include Business Plus and GCP African American. Mulholland Books, an imprint of Little, Brown and Company, specializes in edgy titles with an element of suspense.

The size and complexity of most trade publishers means more metadata to create and maintain and regular metadata feeds to multiple partners. The advantage of a standard like ONIX is that metadata can be created and managed in a standardized form that's likely to be suitable for most or all recipients.

Professional and Scholarly Publishers

These publishers produce books, journals, and other materials intended for the scholarly community and for professionals in a wide variety of areas including medicine, law, business, technology, science, and the humanities. The scientific, technical, and medical publishing subset of professional and scholarly publishing is often referred to as "STM." Professional societies as publishers and university presses are included in this group. This segment accounts for about 13 percent of the market.

Challenges

Professional and scholarly books are aimed at highly specialized and sophisticated consumers. Academic libraries and research organizations purchase many scholarly publications and often select and order through suppliers that maintain dedicated library services.

The specialized needs of scholarly and professional readers and the rigorous selection criteria of academic libraries make it important that the metadata is as complete and granular as possible.

The special metadata needs of libraries as consumers are discussed in the subsection on **Libraries** below.

Many large publishers such as Springer, Elsevier, Wiley, and Taylor and Francis, are part of this group, but some publishers in this segment are small in comparison to these examples and large trade houses. In the section below on **Small and Independent Publishers,** we discuss metadata challenges and solutions for small publishers.

We should note that one of the biggest challenges for the professional and scholarly publishing community is maintaining metadata related to journals and other continuing resources. Metadata for serials is not covered in this *Handbook*.

Educational Publishers

Educational publishers produce textbooks and other learning materials such as workbooks, tests, software, and maps. A recent article from *Wired* states: "The biggest publishers in the world today are education publishers." The major educational publishers dwarf trade publishers and media companies in size. Elementary and high school educational materials comprise the second-largest publishing segment by net volume, with around 30 percent of the market.

Textbook marketing, sales channels, and selection are different from those for other types of publishing. K-12 textbooks must meet state standards in order to be considered for adoption so criteria for selection and purchase are closely tied to those standards. A local school board usually votes to decide which textbooks are chosen from a list approved by the state Department of Education. There is a move to Common Core Standards across states so this aspect of selling textbooks is evolving. College and university textbooks may be chosen by the professor or by the department.

Educational publishers rely heavily on regional sales representatives and books are also sold through textbook divisions of large wholesalers or through wholesalers specializing in educational materials. Because of the specialized nature of the educational publishing process, this *Handbook* applies to this segment only to the extent that metadata standards and practices apply to the creation and distribution of metadata for textbooks. Their challenges include the shift to digital resources and the emergence of new internet-based sellers.

Small and Independent Publishers

The terms "small publisher" and "independent publisher" are often used interchangeably. The industry defines "small" publishers as those with sales between $500,000 and $5,000,000 and "very small" publishers as those with sales of $500,000 or less. Bowker defines a "small press" as publishing 100-499 titles each year. Small publishers are often independent as well, meaning they are not part of a large publishing or media organization.

Traditionally, small publishers were also defined as those publishing ten titles or fewer each year. The inexpensive nature of digital technology has made it possible for more small publishers to enter the market and expand the number of titles offered.

Challenges

Small and independent publishers' management systems are often built using Excel, internal databases, or other tools that aren't fully integrated and require lots of manual intervention. This can make it difficult for small publishers to create the type of streamlined and efficient metadata processes that ensure timely and consistent distribution of quality metadata to sales outlets. And yet getting metadata right and distributing it early in the publishing cycle give small and independent publishers an advantage in competing with larger publishers.

If the publisher releases only one or two titles a year, doesn't maintain a significant backlist, and works with only a few trading partners, it may be just as efficient to use the forms provided by Amazon, Barnes & Noble, and other online sellers on a title-by-title basis. Even if the process is manual, it's important to understand the metadata elements desired by these suppliers and to enter data fully, accurately, and in keeping with best practices for product description. The resellers request these data elements because they contribute to better discovery and more sales—the desired result for the seller as well as for the publisher.

In response to publishers' challenges with metadata formatting and distribution, several players have emerged that offer products and services to manage metadata on behalf of publishers. These products and services are discussed in the **Metadata Management Vendors** section of this chapter. This can be a good option for small and independent publishers, saving staff time and ensuring consistent metadata distribution. But the challenges of getting metadata right are essentially challenges of business process and organization rather than technology challenges. Metadata formatted and distributed by metadata management partners is only as good as the original product information created and provided by the publisher.

Self-Publishers

Self-publishing is the publication of a book by the author without a third-party publisher. In part due to the rise of less expensive digital technology, easy-to-use publishing platforms, and increased user acceptance of digital content, self-publishing is the fastest-growing category in the industry. Self-publishers are very interested in learning to use metadata as a part of effective marketing and sales. The basic principles for creating good metadata also apply to self-publishers. However, many self-publishing systems and bookselling platforms for self-published content are outside established publisher supply chain models for metadata distribution and this creates some of the following challenges.

Challenges

The growth of this segment has resulted in many new industry players and an explosion of new titles (and metadata) in the marketplace. The metadata options may vary across publishing/bookselling platforms and often require manual entry of metadata. This means that self-publishers must be careful to take full advantage of all metadata options offered by a vendor and to be consistent in the metadata provided when selling a book through multiple vendors. Some platforms allow authors to bypass the ISBN registration process, resulting in the failure of these self-published titles to be listed in major industry databases of available books. Lack of ISBNs also makes it difficult to accurately report on the size of this publishing category.

The issues and challenges for this segment are important and the effect on overall metadata in the publishing industry is significant. As a result, this Handbook includes a chapter in Part 3 on **Metadata for Self-Publishers and Small Publishers** designed to answer questions and address challenges specific to this segment.

Digital Publishing

By its very nature, digital publishing disrupts traditional supply chain processes related to the distribution of physical items, including metadata distribution. It's possible to publish almost totally outside traditional models of production and bookselling. The rise of internet-only sellers and the subsequent development of new technologies and products that make digital reading more attractive contribute to the continued growth and acceptance of ebooks.

Traditional publishers have entered this space in full force, converting existing books to digital formats and beginning simultaneous publication of new books in print and digital versions. Booksellers also developed technology for reading ebooks and platforms to deliver ebooks to readers. That said, after surging to around 12 percent of format share from 2008-2012, the growth of digital publishing has stalled over the past year or so and remains at around 12 percent.

Challenges

This market is evolving quickly with accompanying business challenges and threats to established players. New entrants to this space may not understand the multiple uses of metadata in bookselling that are crucial to effective marketing and sales. They may see it as relatively insignificant byproduct of digital production rather than as a business asset in and of itself requiring standardization and quality control. Their systems may not support the needs of data exchange in the publishing landscape.

The rise of digital publishing has serious implications for metadata as well as for ebook production, distribution, and sales. For publishers, this new type of book, often produced outside established production functions and workflow and through external technology and systems, results in some loss of control over the product and product metadata. Options for carrying metadata within the ebook package are also evolving and must be considered as part of the publication process.

The conversion of existing titles to digital has contributed to the explosion of content and accompanying metadata that must be shared and managed. Ebook conversions are dealt with outside the normal publishing process, and publishers' internal databases sometimes aren't used for ebook metadata. As a result, metadata released into the marketplace as part of the conversion process is often less than adequate, not informed by industry standards, and inconsistent with metadata for the physical book.

Ideally, publishers will begin to see this as an opportunity as well as a challenge. It can be an opportunity to develop more efficient and consistent workflows and metadata practices for all products in coordination with digital technology partners. It's also an opportunity to rethink supply chain needs and to incorporate new types of processes and entrants to publishing into the overall supply chain dynamic rather than forcing their products and services into existing models that were not designed to accommodate them.

Chapter 9, **Optimizing Product Metadata for Digital Content**, and Chapter 10, **Metadata in Digital Content Files**, address metadata issues specific to digital publishing in more detail. And, although the *Handbook* does not specifically cover production, major vendors in this space are listed in the **Vendor Directory**, with directory listings indicating whether or not the vendor is able to output metadata in ONIX format.

Book Data Aggregators

Book Data Aggregators compile metadata from publishers and other sources and create products and services built on the metadata. Some aggregation products and services are created and sold by the same organizations that serve as the nation's ISBN Agency, giving them immediate access to information about all books for which an ISBN is requested. Bowker, in the United States, and Nielsen, in the United Kingdom, fall into this category. National ISBN Registration Agencies are described in Chapter 5, **National and International Standards Organizations.**

These businesses are data-only and do not engage in bookselling. Their products include data feeds, print and online resources, such as Bowker's *Books In Print®*, and data analytics services.

Others actively compile, enhance, and package book data as a separate business outside the ISBN registration process, providing ongoing data feeds to supplement industry databases. The U.S. wholesaler Ingram Book maintains a comprehensive title database and supports a data service. The database drives Ingram's proprietary search, discovery, and purchasing tools but is also sold as data feeds to retailers and other industry players.

Each of these organizations invests significant staff, technology, and funds to normalize, correct, and enhance publisher metadata. The databases they maintain are huge and are constantly in flux via multiple data feeds from publishers and other sources, automated data manipulation, and staff intervention.

Although Nielsen BookData and Bowker Global Books in Print also cover Canadian titles, capture of book data at the point of ISBN assignment is handled differently in Canada. The Canadian ISBN service is administered by Library and Archives Canada.

BookNet Canada, a not-for-profit industry organization, provides Biblionet, a data aggregation service supplying ONIX metadata back to publishers, distributors, retailers, and other supply chain partners. More information about BookNet Canada is provided in Chapter 12, **Metadata Best Practices and Industry Organizations**. The **Vendor Directory** provides additional information on data aggregators.

Library Metadata Aggregators

The electronic metadata that drives library catalogs and integrated management systems is carried and stored in MARC (MAchine Readable Cataloging). There are specific rules for description and designated fields for types of data.

As with wholesalers, distributors, and retailers, libraries attempt to avoid duplicate record creation for the same titles by using existing MARC records. Vendors serving the library market also need to provide MARC records to their library customers along with book orders. The **Libraries** section below gives more information about library metadata and the challenges it can create for book vendors.

The major creators and providers of MARC records for English-language titles are The Library of Congress in the United States, Library and Archives Canada, and the British Library. Records contained in these databases are available to libraries through direct search, as the database component of library integrated management systems, and through ongoing data feeds purchased by library vendors and organizations serving the library market.

OCLC, a worldwide library cooperative, maintains WorldCat, a huge database consisting of OCLC member-contributed MARC records and MARC records from the Library of Congress and many national libraries, including Library and Archives Canada and the British Library. WorldCat contains over three million bibliographic records and tracks the holdings of over seventy thousand libraries worldwide.

OCLC member libraries and organizations have access to records through direct search and download and through OCLC services built on the data. Record use through direct search and download using OCLC cataloging tools or record retrieval and download via batch services are priced as a subscription service, based on the average number of records the library downloads during the year. There are restrictions on library use and reuse of the records after download into their own library systems.

The public can view WorldCat records for no charge while using WorldCat.org to find books in their local libraries.

Some OCLC services allow vendors or publishers to deliver WorldCat records in coordination with library orders. Other uses of records by for-profit companies are decided on a case-by-case basis with agreements in place between OCLC and the vendor.

Wholesalers, Distributors, and Ebook Aggregators

In general, the vendors covered in this section are business-to-business or business-to-library providers. They serve as intermediaries in moving content (print or digital) and metadata to retailers and libraries where book data is then exposed in consumer-facing interfaces. There are some exceptions in the ebook space, and we'll discuss those as we move through the section. Some vendors are mentioned specifically here in the context of describing the categories of players and providing examples. A list of vendors in this space can be found in the *Handbook*'s **Vendor Directory**.

Wholesalers

Wholesalers' primary customers are retailers and libraries. Traditionally, wholesalers maintain inventory of multiple titles from multiple publishers in quantities that support order fulfillment for multiple retailers and libraries. Retailers and libraries can thus accomplish one-stop shopping for a large percentage of books selected for purchase.

The warehousing of large inventory and fulfillment of orders for books from many publishers creates significant supply-chain efficiencies. Publishers can "outsource" some operational and logistical functions to wholesalers.

In addition to warehousing, order processing, and shipping, wholesalers provide many value-added services to their customers. Most of these are built on metadata. Web-based ordering platforms, such as Baker & Taylor's Title Source™ and Ingram's ipage®, offer many ways to sort and view titles for selection, including sorting by category, age range, demand, publication date, and combinations of these and other data points.

Wholesalers also use data to generate selection lists and approval plans for retailers and libraries based on criteria provided by the customer in complex and detailed profiles. Available titles can be compared to titles already present in existing stores or libraries to generate new store or library selection lists.

Metadata must be complete and correct if the automation used to sort titles and generate lists is to present titles for selection that meet customer needs. Titles with missing or inaccurate metadata may never be exposed to the buyer as candidates for purchase. Major wholesalers invest in making metadata better and have processes in place for quality control and data enhancement. Title data ultimately viewed within the wholesalers' products and services is often altered from the original data received from the publisher.

Distributors

While wholesalers provide materials and services to retailers and libraries, distributors act as a link between publishers and retailers. Although distributors do facilitate sales to retailers and libraries, publishers are their customers and distributors specifically represent publisher interests and activities.

Distributors may specialize in a particular type of publisher — small, independent, or regional, for example — or they may specialize in publishers of certain types or genres of books, such as graphic novels or crafts books.

Distributors also maintain databases of the titles they promote and provide data feeds to retailers. Metadata plays a big part in marketing and selling the books of the publishers they represent.

Ebook Aggregators and Distributors

This space is evolving quickly with many new entrants to the playing field and established supply chain players' continued development of services focused on digital resources. We don't claim to provide comprehensive coverage of the challenges surrounding ebook aggregation, distribution, retailing, and library lending but instead point to implications and challenges relating to the creation and distribution of metadata.

Ebook Aggregators

The term "ebook aggregator" is commonly used to talk about a category of vendors that emerged fairly early in the digital revolution to provide ebooks and other electronic resources to libraries. These companies do not generally distribute into the retail market. Major players include OverDrive, ebrary (a Proquest company), and MyiLibrary® (owned by Ingram).

Ebook aggregators offer libraries digital resources from multiple publishers, providing platforms that allow access to library patrons. Metadata is used in the library selection process but also powers the platforms from which readers discover and select titles to borrow. Ebook aggregators in the library space are also expected to provide title records in MARC format to populate library catalogs (databases) that require book data in MARC format. For more information about the data implications of selling to libraries, see the **Libraries** section below.

Ebook Distributors

For the purposes of this book, we distinguish ebook distributors from aggregators as vendors distributing into the retail market. Distribution into retail outlets such as Apple, Amazon, and Barnes & Noble is usually offered along with ebook production and/or conversion, and the vendors may also support direct-to-consumer sales from their websites.

Many of the new industry players are in this space, including companies such as Smashwords, Lulu, and BookBaby. They are strongly focused on self-publishing and small publishers. With the growth of self-publishing, these new players have introduced a significant amount of metadata into the marketplace.

Initial metadata comes directly from the author (as publisher) and may not be consistent with publishing industry best practices and standards. In fact, the metadata tools and platforms provided by new players might not support the level of metadata needed to effectively expose and sell self-published titles in a market crowded with books and metadata.

Traditional publishers also turn to new vendors for conversion of new and backlist titles to digital formats. When metadata produced from this process (often completely separated from metadata workflow for print) enters the marketplace without thorough review for completeness, quality, and consistency with print versions of the title, search, discovery, sales, and business intelligence suffer.

The BISG study *The Development, Use, and Modification of Book Product Metadata* identifies better communication and collaboration with new market entrants as an opportunity for improvement in book product metadata.

Retailers

We visit their stores; we browse and buy on their websites — for most of the reading public, retail booksellers are taken for granted as part of our lives. But most of us are also aware of the transformation in bookselling precipitated by the rise of internet-only sellers and the increased reader embrace of content in digital form.

Metadata plays a big role in this transformation. Since most retail booksellers now also maintain a web store, metadata that starts with a publisher (or author) and moves through the intermediaries described above will eventually be exposed on a platform from which the reader selects and buys books. For continued bookselling from bricks-and-mortar retail outlets, metadata is essential for making sound decisions when buying from wholesalers and distributors, but metadata also plays a role in inventory, merchandising, and sales tracking for books sold from a physical location.

Challenges

Large retailers must maintain title databases that support all the metadata uses mentioned above. Many invest significant staff and technology resources to the capture, maintenance, and manipulation of metadata. As with the intermediaries, changes to the metadata can occur here to ensure that book data meets the needs of the retailers' systems, merchandising and marketing strategies, and desired website experience for customers.

Independent Bookstores

These bookstores are independently owned and are not controlled by a larger bookseller chain. They are usually strongly integrated with and responsive to the communities they serve. Buying choices are not decided at a corporate level but are strongly influenced by the bookstore's individual brand and mission along with the needs and wants of its readers.

Independent bookstores can be as broad as or broader than chains in titles offered and can have a strong web presence. Titles offered may include used as well new ones. Powell's Books, based in Portland, Oregon, markets itself as "the largest independent new and used bookstore in the world." Its website offers an experience similar to websites maintained by chains, with the ability to browse based on many criteria, including category, format, new or used, and publication date.

Other independents cater to niche markets and are very focused in the type of titles they carry. Owners and staff have a specific area of expertise with a deep knowledge of their books and their readers.

Challenges

Independents buy from mainstream wholesalers and retailers but may also buy from unusual sources to meet readers' expectations. Their metadata needs for buying and selling may go beyond the usual as well, and they do not benefit from the technology and infrastructure maintained by corporate retailers. Decisions regarding data sources and data maintenance tools are made by the individual store and have an impact on operating expenses and revenue.

Chain Bookstores

We know that many independents failed to survive during the period of retail chain store expansion. But most of us didn't predict that chain stores would face similar challenges resulting from Amazon's entry into bookselling and the rise of online selling in general.

Just as large retail outlets experienced benefits from the sheer number of stores easily available to readers and from supply chain efficiencies not possible for smaller independents, chain retailers found themselves in competition with new retailers that found ways to increase efficiency and grow market share by creating a new way to shop for books.

Challenges

Chain retailers developed their own websites to meet reader demand for online shopping options. Metadata used for buying, inventory control, merchandising, and sales tracking now must take center stage on retailer websites offering online shopping in competition with Amazon and other Internet sellers. Metadata is now fully exposed to the user as the means by which they select and buy books. Better and more complete metadata is required to support online buying and retailers invested in the technology and expertise required to manage a successful user experience.

Online Retailers

The challenge posed to traditional bookstores by Amazon and other online-only retailers was described above. While bricks-and-mortar booksellers moved to create online options, Amazon had already invested heavily in metadata, website development, search and discovery options, and algorithms that also analyzed user behavior to expose the right titles to the right readers.

The role of metadata in online bookselling cannot be emphasized enough. It is the reader's experience of shopping for books. Aspects of bookselling such as merchandising and shelving by category now happen online. Reader perusal of information on the book jacket or inside a physical book — descriptions, author information, reviewer quotes and awards, tables of contents, cover design — must be replicated online.

Challenges

This requires metadata to be organized and stored in a way that facilitates both user-driven search and discovery and the algorithms that present titles to users without a specific search. Book metadata that includes enough information to identify and suggest similar titles is behind automated decisions to display some books to readers, and inadequate metadata results in the exclusion of other books that might actually fit the criteria.

Online shopping also allows visibility of many more titles than can usually be accommodated in a bricks-and-mortar store. This provides more opportunity for sales but produces more metadata to manage. Attention to metadata quality along with sound metadata practices and management can help create a competitive advantage for any type of bookseller.

Libraries

Traditionally, large wholesalers, sometimes called "book jobbers," with divisions created to meet the needs of the library market, serve libraries. Libraries come in many types and sizes and comprise a complex market with selection and buying practices that can be quite different from retailers. The types of materials bought differ widely between public libraries, academic libraries, and special libraries. The nature of value-added services required, such as classification for shelving and physical processing, can also be significantly different, even between libraries of the same type.

Libraries generally use vendor metadata, ordering systems, and services to select books and place orders. But in order to meet library demand for "shelf-ready" materials, library service vendors are also often required to provide an entirely different type of metadata along with book orders. Libraries were among the first to develop online systems (catalogs) for data/inventory management and user search. Migration from card catalogs to electronic bibliographic records began in the early 1980s, long before the rise of online reader access to book information for bookselling.

Library systems for electronic catalogs are built on book information packaged in MARC (MAchine Readable Cataloging) format, a metadata structure introduced in the late 1960s. Full-scale library migration from card catalogs to electronic bibliographic records in MARC format began in the 1970s, long before the rise of online reader access to book information for bookselling.

Libraries also use complex classification systems, such as Library of Congress and Dewey Decimal Classification, and controlled subject vocabularies. Refer to the section on **Book Industry Metadata Standards** for more information about the MARC standard.

Challenges

The data that vendors receive from publishers and use in their own systems does not fully meet the needs of libraries. Library vendors often maintain parallel databases of MARC records, purchasing data feeds from the Library of Congress and national libraries to populate the databases. The largest vendors also maintain a staff of library professionals to create MARC records for books without a record in the MARC data feeds and to adapt existing MARC records to the specifications of individual libraries.

Whether this duplication of efforts related to book metadata is sustainable is up for debate. The library community is exploring new ideas about metadata and migration away from the MARC format. This may open up opportunities for libraries and the publishing industry to make better use of the same metadata. In the meantime, library customers present metadata challenges for the vendors that serve them. Libraries and vendors also face challenges in the purchase, use, and management of digital resources in libraries.

Metadata Management Vendors

Managing metadata internally and handling the distribution of multiple data files to multiple partners can be a challenge for publishers. Proprietary and legacy systems developed internally over the years often prove inadequate for 21st century metadata management.

This section applies to vendors providing a product, service, or component that assists publishers in the management of title metadata, including the ability to create and export metadata files to trading partners. They may also be called "title management" or "content management" systems or services.

Some companies developed products specifically designed to handle publisher metadata, transforming it to the ONIX standard when needed and adapting data files to meet trading partner specifications. Unfortunately, not all recipient systems are built to optimize even the best and most standardized files and demand that certain elements are added to or changed in files before they are accepted. Publishers want their titles listed in as many channels as possible, and the internal creation of multiple files can be labor-intensive.

Companies such as Firebrand (Eloquence), Onixsuite, NetRead, and ONIXEdit, offer ONIX data creation, conversion, and distribution tools and services. BookNet Canada also offers "Biblio Tools" to help publishers create and manage ONIX files. These services can be especially valuable for small or midsized publishers that choose not to invest in a multifunction, integrated publishing management system.

Metadata creation and management functionality, including the ability to export and distribute data feeds to multiple partners, is a component of many larger integrated management systems. Publishing Technology, Klopotek, and Virtusales are examples of this category, offering production tools and business solutions as well as a metadata component. Firebrand also offers content and business management tools as well as ONIX solutions. It's important for publishers to make sure the system chosen provides this functionality. Check to see that a full range of data elements can be captured and stored and that ONIX export is supported. See the **Vendor Directory** for a list of business management and metadata management vendors.

Part 2: Book Industry Metadata Standards

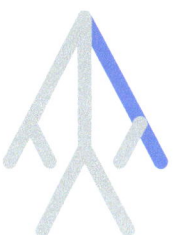

Chapter 3: A Brief History of Metadata Standards and Practices

Early Libraries

Book metadata is as least as old as the Library at Alexandria, constructed in the 3rd century BC. The approximately 500,000 works held in the Library were inventoried and assigned to subject categories. Book information was recorded in the *Pinakes*, the first known library catalog.

A typical entry included the book's title, the author's name and birthplace, his father's name, any teachers he trained under, his educational background, a brief biography, and a list of the author's publications. The first line of the work, a summary of its contents, and information about the origin of the work could also be included. Works were housed in separate rooms according to subject. Variations on the *Pinakes* system were used until the late 1800s.

The Printing Press

Practices of metadata and knowledge organization and the creation of manuscript lists stayed firmly within the purview of libraries and monasteries until the invention of the printing press around 1440. Books became accessible to more than the wealthy and scholarly population and demand grew. Private presses flourished and publishing output increased to more than 20 million volumes by the year 1500.

Industrialization and the Birth of Modern Publishing

Thomas Jefferson maintained a manuscript list for his collection of 6,700 books, which were sold to the U.S. Congress in 1815, marking the birth of the Library of

Congress. Catalogs such as Jefferson's manuscript list remained common even as a fundamental transformation in publishing (and book metadata standards) occurred in the mid-19th century. Mechanization and industrialization changed the way books were made and sold.

Many of today's major publishing houses were founded in the 19th century. You can still see the basic elements of book description from the Alexandrian Library echoed in printed publisher catalogs that remained, until recently, one of the principal ways information about books for sale was shared. Most included title, author, subject, summary, information about the maker (publisher), and the date published.

The elements considered necessary for publisher catalogs were similar and generally accepted across publishers, but there was no real industry standard for publisher book data. The *Annual American Catalog*, published in 1870, represented movement toward standardized book data. Convinced that good bibliographic information was necessary for efficient book business, Frederick Leypoldt, a German immigrant and bookseller, published the *Catalog*. It was the precursor to *Books in Print*®. R.R. Bowker later acquired Leypoldt's company, and the company still bears his name.

Formal Metadata Standards and Practices

A major move toward new standards and practices came from the library community. There was a great deal of activity in library standards from the mid-19th century into the late 1960s. This period saw the invention of the Dewey Decimal System, Library of Congress Classification, and Library of Congress Subject Headings.

Codifying of rules for entering book data emerged in the *British Museum Rules* (1841), *Cutter's Rules* (1876) and the evolution of cataloging rules in America and the United Kingdom from 1908 through the publication of the *Anglo-American Cataloging Rules (AACR)* in 1967. During this period catalog cards served as the major mechanism for describing, organizing, and locating books.

The International Standard Book Description (ISBD) rules for printed monographs were published in 1971. ISBD identifies the components of a bibliographic description along with preferred order and punctuation. A chapter of AACR was revised in 1971 for consistency with ISBD. AACR experienced further revisions and new editions between 1978 and 2002.

New Standards in Support of Computing

Standards emerging from the late 1960s through the 1970s reflect the movement toward electronic records and electronic (machine-to-machine) data exchange enabled by the increasing adoption of mainframe computer systems in libraries and in the publisher supply chain.

The library community developed the MARC (MAchine Readable Cataloging) record format to allow electronic exchange and online display of data traditionally shown in card catalogs. Library of Congress MARC was introduced in 1967 and UK MARC appeared in 1968. Libraries began to develop Online Public Access systems (OPACs) to replace the card catalog as the main library interface with the public.

In 1965, the United Kingdom's then-dominant book retailer W.H. Smith announced plans to move to computerized warehousing and inventory and commissioned consultants to recommend a standard numbering system. The nine-digit Standard Book Number code (SBN) was implemented in 1967 and was adopted by the International Organization for Standardization (ISO) as the ten-digit International Standard Book Number (ISBN) in 1970. ISBN was expanded to thirteen digits in 1997 to increase the numbering capacity of the system and to align ISBN with the GTIN (Global Trade Item Number) system that is used internationally in the identification of other consumer goods. ISBN is the primary system for book identification in approximately 150 countries.

The ISBN system supported management and tracking of book inventory, but further support for automated electronic commerce was needed. Standards such as X12 and EDIFACT for electronic data interchange (EDI) were designed to automate commercial communication between businesses. The growth of large wholesalers and retail chains requiring extensive messaging between a growing number of players made the ability to communicate electronically essential.

The bibliographic information (descriptive information about the book) contained in inventory databases and transmitted electronically supported internal operations and commercial transactions. Book data was not exposed to the consumer and could be very brief since the ISBN served as the major match point for business communication. Printed catalogs and other selling tools contained extensive information but the catalogs were controlled, produced, and edited outside computerized inventory and data transmission systems. Amazon and the rise of Internet bookselling changed everything.

21st Century Libraries and Bookselling

In response to the need for an electronic carrier of rich book information that worked in the world of e-commerce, the publishing industry introduced ONIX for Books in 2000. ONIX is now the international standard for communicating book industry information. An XML-based standard, ONIX is designed for global use across languages and national book trade characteristics.

Although libraries were early to provide an online user experience through MARC records and Online Public Access Catalogs, the underlying rules, data formats, and standards remained fairly static after the massive conversion of catalog cards to electronic records during the 1970s and 1980s. In 2002, the Library of Congress developed MARC-XML to allow better use of MARC records in a web environment.

Also in 2002, the library community began review of AACR. This led to the development of a new approach designed to better meet the needs of the digital world. Resource Description and Access (RDA) was conceived in 2005, published in 2010, and was fully implemented by the Library of Congress in 2013, replacing the current version of AACR for the creation of new records.

In 2011, the Library of Congress began the process of determining a transition path away from the MARC-21 standard. The project is being carried out in coordination with Library and Archives Canada, the British Library, Deutsche Nationalbibliothek, and other national libraries, agencies, library vendors, and committees. In 2012, LC announced a strong focus on transitioning to a Linked Data model. Specifics of the move from AACR to RDA and from MARC 21 to a new data format indicate a greater consideration of integration and interactivity between library and publisher metadata.

The explosion of titles (both new titles and converted backlist titles) and ebook formats resulting from the rise of digital publishing creates new challenges for standardization. A huge increase in self-publishing and print-on-demand publishers along with the transition to digital in traditional publishing present problems in the sheer volume of metadata to manage as well as additional data streams from new industry players.

The ONIX for Books standard continues to evolve in response to the changing market. Released in 2009, ONIX 3.0 expands options for describing digital products and addresses emerging metadata needs relating to commerce. Potential uses for newer identifier standards such as ISTC (International Standard Text Code) and ISNI (International Standard Name Identifier) are under consideration within the industry. These and other important book industry standards are described in the following chapter.

Industry organizations are engaged in research to map the current landscape and are revising documentation to reflect metadata requirements for ebooks and new ways of selling. Publishing appears to be in a period of active response to emerging demands and possibilities similar to the industry's reaction to the rise of computing in business during the 1960s and 1970s.

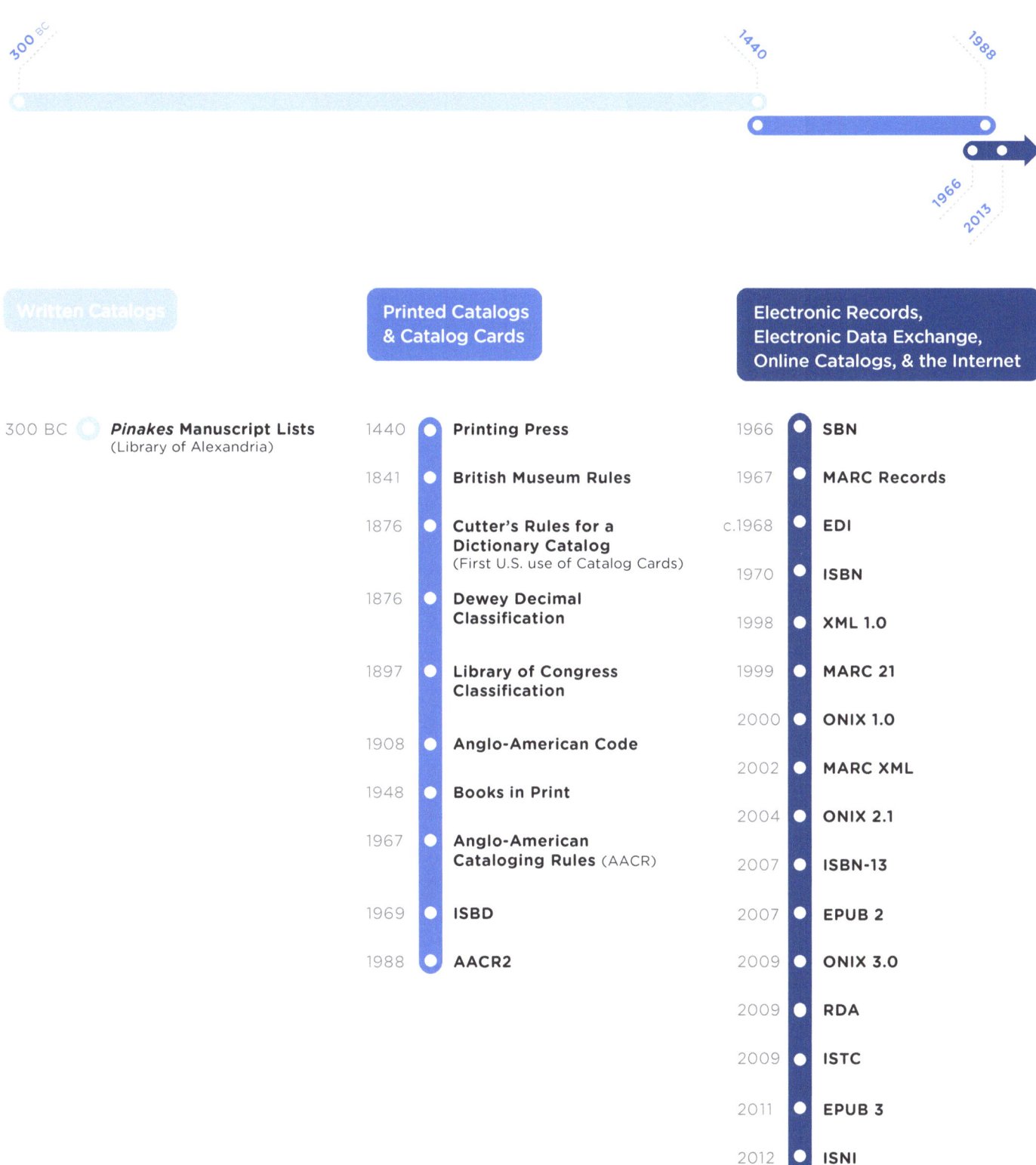

Chapter 4: Book Industry Standards for Sharing Metadata

The previous chapter outlines the evolution of metadata standards for books and publishing. The shift to electronic communication between businesses required that industry players find an efficient way to "talk" machine-to-machine. Machine-to-machine communication increases efficiency and speed, but there isn't a lot of room for clarification in this communication process. It was essential to develop a common "language" with shared terminology, definitions, grammar, and structure so that machines could understand and interpret messages in a consistent way.

The need for structured data that is shared using agreed-on standards is certainly not unique to publishing. Each industry has terminology, identifiers, and other types of information specific to that business. There are engineering data standards, automotive product data standards, standards for product data in the healthcare supply chain and the list goes on. This chapter covers some of the major standards used to share information about books.

ISBN and Other Identifiers

In electronic communications and data processing, numeric identifiers often stand in for information in text form. Following are descriptions of several identifiers specific to or especially relevant to book metadata. The agencies responsible for administration of publishing industry identifiers are covered in Chapter 5.

ISBN (International Standard Book Number)

The ability to consistently and reliably identify a particular product across multiple trading partner systems is essential to electronic business communication. As discussed in Chapter 3, the ISBN was developed in the mid-1960s and accepted as the industry-standard identifier for books in the 1970s. The International Standards Organization (ISO) developed the system and the first edition of ISBN (ISO Standard 2108) was published in 1972.

When applied correctly, each ISBN is unique to an individual product. The ISBN then provides a reliable product reference number and match point for data exchange about a particular book product. The term "book product" is used here because the ISBN does not apply to every instance of the book's core content — the "work." The "work" *Moby-Dick* has generated many different "book products" in multiple formats and editions (hardcover, paperback, audio, digital, annotated editions, illustrated editions, translations, and more), with multiple publishers. Effective selling requires that each of these products be uniquely identified.

The ISBN was developed to replace the in-house numbering systems emerging in the mid-1960s as computer technology began to be used for sharing business information. Continued expansion of in-house numbering systems for each supplier would have inhibited rather than enhanced the potential for machine-to-machine transaction. With proprietary, in-house systems, multiple identifiers would be used to reference the same book product, or one identifier was used for multiple products, creating administrative problems for publishers and confusion in the marketplace. The ISBN could be assigned early in the publishing process and then "belong" to the publisher and the book, traveling with the book throughout buying and selling activities. Vendors might still maintain in-house numbering systems for internal business reasons and uses, but the ISBN would remain unique to the book and keep the same meaning across multiple systems.

As is implicit in its name, International Standard Book Number, ISBN is still the standard for identifying a book product across countries and systems. It has expanded over the years to accommodate the growing number of titles published and requiring a unique identifier for commerce. The first through third ISBN editions used a 10-digit identifier.

The fourth edition, published in May 2005, expanded the ISBN to 13 digits, and from January 2007 onward, all ISBNs issued conformed to the 13-digit standard. The main reason for expansion was to increase capacity. But at the same time, the ISBN also merged with the 13-digit universal product code system then known as EAN (European Article Number), now known as the GTIN-13 (Global Trade Item Number).

The ISBN Users' Manual is available for download in PDF format on the International ISBN Agency website and offers extensive guidelines for when to apply an ISBN. Section 5.1 of the Manual provides a general statement of rules for ISBN application:

> A separate ISBN shall be applied to each separate monographic publication or separate edition or format of a monographic publication issued by a publisher. A separate ISBN shall be assigned to each different language edition of a monographic publication.

Section 5.1 states that new ISBNs should be applied to different formats of the same book. Section 5.4, "Publications in different product forms," explains further:

> Different product forms of a publication (e.g. hardback, paperback, Braille, audiobook, online electronic publication) require separate ISBNs. Where electronic publications are made available in different file formats each separately available file format shall be assigned a unique ISBN.

The rapid expansion in the number of file formats for ebooks (and other electronic resources), along with widespread acceptance of the ebook in general, resulted in new issues for publishers and sellers. A greater number of ISBNs are needed to represent the various ebook formats released along with traditional formats. Conversion of backlist titles to digital products also results in the need for additional ISBNs and more metadata to manage.

Under ISBN application guidelines, it's now necessary to obtain multiple ISBNs when publishers offer a book in multiple ebook formats. Industry organizations, including the IAA and the Book Industry Study Group (BISG), addressed confusion around ISBN application for digital publications by publishing policy statements. This issue and current policies are discussed further in Part 3, **Essential Metadata Elements**. For the foreseeable future, the industry will continue to analyze and respond to the implications of digital publishing and electronic distribution of content for the publisher supply chain. Publishers should be alert to evolving standards and best practices surrounding digital publishing and bookselling.

As a complete number, the ISBN refers to a specific publication, but the numbers comprising the ISBN have meaning as well. The hyphens and spaces sometimes seen in ISBNs are not actually part of the ISBN. These may be inserted to make the number more readable. The positioning of the hyphens varies, as the number of digits used in each of the groups 1–4 varies (always adding up to 12 digits between them).

There are five groups of numbers within the 13-digit ISBN as shown in the following example.

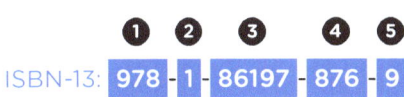

ISBN-13: 978 - 1 - 86197 - 876 - 9

1. Prefix Element
2. Registration Group Element
3. Registrant Element
4. Publication Element
5. Check Digit

1. Prefix Element
ISBN-13: **978** - 1 - 86197 - 876 - 9

The *prefix* allows the ISBN to be integrated into the wider global product identification system, making the ISBN in a GTIN-13. Two new prefixes (978 and 979) were made available by GS1, the global standards organization. 978 prefixes allowed systems to contain both ISBN-10 and ISBN-13. Once 978 prefixes were exhausted and the 979 prefix was utilized, ISBN-10 equivalents were no longer allowed.

2. Registration Group Element
ISBN-13: 978 - **1** - 86197 - 876 - 9

The *registration group element* refers to the country, geographical, or language area of the publisher.

3. Registrant Element
ISBN-13: 978 - 1 - **86197** - 876 - 9

The *registrant* refers to the publisher or imprint. Publisher prefixes are assigned by the agency issuing the ISBN. National ISBN Registry Agencies are discussed in Chapter 5.

4. Publication Element
ISBN-13: 978 - 1 - 86197 - **876** - 9

The *publication element* refers to a specific publication by that publisher.

5. Check Digit
ISBN-13: 978 - 1 - 86197 - 876 - **9**

The *check digit* completes the ISBN. A check digit serves as a redundancy or error check for systems using the ISBN. It is automatically calculated from the preceding numbers and so can be "checked" and validated automatically by the system receiving the number.

ISNI (International Standard Name Identifier)

As described at isni.org, this identifier " ... is the ISO certified global standard number for identifying the millions of contributors to creative works and those active in their distribution, including researchers, inventors, writers, artists, visual creators, performers, producers, publishers, aggregators, and more." This unique identifier disambiguates different forms of a name. It allows all works by a contributor to be grouped together, regardless of how the name is expressed on packaging of a work. Examples of issues resolved by ISNI include:

- Differences in spelling of author names, such as Tolstoy and Tolstoi
- Pseudonyms for the same contributor, Stephen King writing as Richard Bachman, for example
- Contributors with the same or similar names, such as John Smith, early American explorer and captain, and John Smith, author of *10 Easy Ways to Make Money Online*.

By allowing reliable linking to content across multiple metadata sources, ISNI contributes to a better and more accurate search experience. Consistent application of this standard also has the potential to clarify royalty and licensing payments.

There are currently records for over eight million identities. Registration agencies are appointed by the international agency and include Bowker and Bibliotheque national de France.

ISTC (International Standard Text Code)

Unlike the ISBN, the ISTC identifies a "work" rather than a "product." A relatively recent standard, ISTC was published as an ISO standard (ISO-21047) in 2009. In the section on ISBN, we described ISBN as an identifier registered by and "belonging to" a publisher. The ISTC "belongs" to the work it identifies regardless of the publisher or format of a particular product.

Using the same example as for ISBN, *Moby-Dick*, the work by Herman Melville, would be assigned an ISTC. The ISTC would remain the same for *Moby-Dick* as published by any publisher, and in paperback, hardcover, or digital format. The ISTC essentially identifies the content. If the content is changed — is translated into another language or abridged, for example — then a new ISTC should be assigned.

Where the ISBN's main value is in the identification of products and the facilitation of electronic commerce, the ISTC serves to enhance the effectiveness of metadata and improve discoverability in a search environment. Internet retail booksellers and wholesalers find it valuable to expose different versions of the same title in search results. This can be harder than it appears when attempting to bring like things together using only the text in the records.

An Amazon search on *Moby-Dick* in books does return a lot of books that really are *Moby-Dick* by Herman Melville. But on the very first page of results, it also returns *Why Read Moby-Dick* by Nathanial Philbrick.

SAN (Standard Address Number)

R.R. Bowker developed the SAN system and Bowker serves as the U.S. SAN Agency. SANs are unique identifiers assigned to addresses or organizations involved in book selling and publishing. SAN is an American National Standard but the U.S. SAN Agency assigns SANs to locations in the U.S., Canada, and all other locations outside the U.S. with the exceptions of Australia, New Zealand, and the U.K. Nielsen Book serves as the SAN Agency for these locations.

SANs are used to accurately identify participants in commercial transactions such as those between publishers and booksellers. Their purpose is to reduce errors in ordering, billing, shipping, and other common transactions. SAN registration is common for organizations that engage in these types of transactions frequently. Examples include book publishers, wholesalers, libraries and library systems, printers, binders, and other vendors providing an industry-related business function.

LCCN (Library of Congress Control Number)

The LCCN is a unique number assigned by the Library of Congress. An LCCN is used to identify a bibliographic record corresponding to a publication and not for commercial product identification purposes, as is the case with ISBN and SAN. It provides a reliable match point in the Library of Congress database and other library databases. Once assigned, it's commonly printed inside the book. It is not the same as copyright registration through the U.S. Copyright Agency.

Only U.S. book publishers are eligible to obtain LCCN, and there is no charge. The LCCN can be assigned before publication, but publishers must send a copy of the book to the Library of Congress immediately upon publication. Though not absolutely necessary, it's helpful to obtain this number if the publisher expects significant sales to the library market.

Metadata Schemes

Metadata schemes define sets of metadata elements used for specific purposes, such as describing and selling books. The structure and rules of the schemes allow metadata elements contained in a structured file (title, author, price, etc.) to be efficiently and accurately distributed, received, and interpreted by multiple players, and correctly displayed in multiple user interfaces.

For example, when publishers format and distribute their metadata in ONIX, the international standard scheme for book metadata, it becomes much easier for major wholesalers and retailers to interpret the metadata and display it on their user-facing websites.

ONIX for Books

ONIX for Books is an XML-based international standard for representing and communicating book product information in electronic form. The standard is designed to allow global communication, without language limitations. It is the most widely used of the ONIX family of products administered by EDItEUR. The ONIX family also includes ONIX for Serials and ONIX for Publications Licenses. ONIX for Books is used in North America, Western Europe, Japan, Russia, parts of Eastern Europe, with early implementations in China and Egypt.

ONIX for Books Release 1.0 was published in 2001 and is now in Release 3.0, published in 2009. Version 2.1, published in 2003, is still in use by some at this writing, but the December 2014 sunset of technical support for ONIX 2.1 makes it urgent that ONIX users transition as soon as possible.

Benefits of Using ONIX

Using a standard data format providing a shared framework of structures, conventions, and codes allows consistent transfer of substantial volumes of complex information about books across the industry.

When senders and receivers use ONIX, manual intervention in file processing is reduced, accuracy of data interpretation is enhanced, and the speed of processing is increased. This is because the systems are essentially speaking the same information "language" and using the same grammar (structure).

ONIX Format and Structure

The ONIX message is written in XML (Extensible Markup Language) and is usually delivered via FTP (File Transfer Protocol). XML was designed to structure, store, and transport data. HTML and XML are both markup languages, but HTML was designed to facilitate web-based display of information whereas XML is a data carrier. XML data tags are not predefined; the user community creating the particular application of XML, in this case ONIX for Books, defines them.

ONIX Tag Names

Human-readable ONIX XML tag names, or reference names, such as `<KeyName>`, are used for all the metadata examples in this *Handbook*. ONIX for Books tag names can also be converted into short tags, resulting in reduced file size. EDItEUR provides an ONIX for Books tagname converter, allowing ONIX reference names to be converted to short tags and vice versa. ONIX users should refer to documentation for any differences in tags between ONIX 2.1 and ONIX 3.0.

The tags in the ONIX message — the reference names of the data elements — are defined as part of the overall structure and allow everyone using ONIX to transmit and translate book product data in a consistent way. The tools used to enter title data in title management systems or databases may not name the data elements in the same way. For example, the title data entry system at a publisher may have the data fields:

First Name
Last Name

While the ONIX message expresses this information as:

```
<NamesBeforeKey>
<KeyName>
```

"Key name" tells the system interpreting the data that this is the name used for indexing, usually the surname. In Chapter 13, **BISG's Best Practices for Product Metadata: Guide for North American Data Senders and Receivers**, the *Handbook* gives further examples of common information about books as structured in ONIX XML format.

Data entry systems that allow effective conversion to ONIX behind the scenes do not have to use the same field names as the ONIX message, but they do need to have defined fields that can be mapped to ONIX. For example, there must be at least two fields to carry name information (first name, last name), or none of the downstream systems will able to index or display the data correctly.

ONIX Code Lists

Understanding the role of ONIX Code Lists is essential to understanding how to communicate using ONIX. Codes are language-independent and so contribute to the effectiveness of ONIX as an international standard.

Using codes to stand in for text increases accuracy and efficiency in data transmission and interpretation. The Code Lists act as controlled vocabularies — each user has the same group of options from which to choose, and the codes mean the same thing across senders, receivers, and their systems, even if the words senders and receivers choose for describing particular options vary.

Code Lists cover many aspects of book description and bookselling including contributor role (roles allowed go far beyond author to include almost any role that can be related to the creation of a work), ISO-defined language and country codes, audience age ranges, sales rights, availability, and product form detail, expanded in version 3.0 to include additional ebook file formats such as EPUB and Mobi, to name just a few.

ONIX for Books Product Information Message

Full information on the ONIX for Books format can be found in the EDItEUR document *ONIX for Books Product Format Specification 3.0.1*, available from the EDItEUR website, and the accompanying *Implementation and Best Practice guide*. This section gives only a high level overview of the ONIX for Books Product Information Message.

Following is a very high-level list of what's included in an ONIX for Books Version 3.0 Message. A brief description of 3.0 changes from Version 2.1 follows the overview. The start of the message is dictated by the rules of the XML standard and is followed by a sequence of XML tags and data specific to the ONIX message.

Message Header

The message Header Composite carries information that applies to the entire record. Components within the Header include:

- Information about the sender of the message
- Information about the intended receiver (addressee) of the message
- Information about the message itself, such as:
  - The date and time the message was created
  - Whether it's a repeat transmission
  - A sequence number if it's one in a series of messages
  - Notes

Product Record

The Product Record is the heart of the ONIX Message, describing various aspects of one product. The entire group of elements beginning, with the XML label `<Product>` and ending with the XML label `</Product>`, is the ONIX product record, and there can be many records within a single ONIX message.

P.1 Record Reference, Type, and Source

A single unique and permanent reference that will be used every time information about the book is sent. This identifier refers to the *record* not the *product*. Best practice dictates that the record reference should not be a product identifier, such as an ISBN. However, the record reference may *include* a product identifier within a longer string of characters.

P.2 Product Numbers

- **Product Identifier**: A valid product identifier is required in every product record. This is usually the ISBN-13 in its unhyphenated form, labeled as an EAN.UCC GTIN-13 number.
- **Barcode**: Optional and only expected to be used in North America.

Block 1: Product Description (P.3 - P.13)

P.3 Product Form

Describes the physical or digital nature of a product. The ONIX tags allow precise description of aspects including whether a book is hardcover, trade or mass-market paperback, or Amazon Kindle ebook; if the primary content is text, map, or audio; if digital content has DRM constraints, and many other form-related aspects.

P.4 Product Parts

Describes the parts of a product consisting of multiple components — a book that comes with a CD, for example.

P.5 Collection

New to version 3.0, *Collection* allows the description of various types of sets, series, and other collections.

P.6 Product Title Detail

Contains the product's title, its subtitle, and other information that may relate to the title.

P.7 Authorship

Allows multiple contributor roles, multiple contributors, and multiple representations of a contributor name, such as an alternate name. *Authorship* also allows information about a contributor, such as birth and death dates, biographical information, professional positions and affiliations, contributor website, and many others.

P.8 Conference

Used if the publication is related to a conference.

P.9 Edition

Carries information about a book's edition including edition number and edition statement. Also provides multiple options for describing complex edition information relating to Bibles and other religious texts.

P.10 Language

Specifies the language used in the product. It can also be used to specify the language of the original work when the product is a translation and to indicate the script in which the language is represented, if applicable.

P.11 Extents and Other Content

Covers number of pages, run times, and other extent designations. Also indicates when other content such as illustrations, bibliography, and index are included.

P.12 Subject

Allows transmission of various types of subjects, including BISAC and BIC subject headings, and keywords.

P.13 Audience

Allows communication of a general target audience, young adult, for example, and audience range, such as U.S. school grade 9 up to grade 12.

Block 2: Marketing Collateral Detail (P.14 - P.17)

P.14 Descriptions and Other Supporting Text

Used for text that is carried in the ONIX record, for example a blurb, an excerpt from a review, or a table of contents. Supporting text that is not embedded within the ONIX record is carried in other sections.

P.15 Cited Content

Carries content cited from a third party, with links to digital sources or references to print sources.

P.16 Links to Supporting Resources

Describes supporting resources and provides links to web addresses. A supporting resource is content in digital form provided by a publisher or other supply chain partner to be used by the receiver for promotional purposes. A typical supporting resource is a JPEG of the front cover of a book.

P.17 Prizes

Carries information about prizes and awards won by the book.

Block 3: Content Detail (P.18)

P.18 Content Items

Used to describe individual parts or chapters within a product in a structured way.

Block 4: Publishing Detail (P.19 - P.21)

Carries information on the imprint, publisher(s), publishing status, and territorial sales rights.

P.19 Publisher

Identifies the publisher and/or imprint (brand) name, city and country of publication, publisher website, and publisher contact for the product.

P.20 Global Publishing Status and Dates/Copyright

Provides the status of a product, such as active or forthcoming, and publishing dates that aren't specific to a geographic market. Copyright information can also be carried.

P.21 Territorial Rights and Other Sales Restrictions

Allows sales rights to be specified for any geographic territory. Sales outlets can also be identified along with any sales restrictions.

Block 5: Related Material (P.22 - P.23)

Allows the publisher or seller to point to products or works related to the product being described in the record.

P.22 Related Works

Allows use of an ISTC to identify the work and related works, the same work in a different format or binding, for example.

P.23 Related Products

Allows use of an ISBN to identify related products, such as other products with the same content, preceding or following edition of the product, and other related products. Only a link to the related product is carried rather than full product detail.

Block 6: Product Supply (P.24 - P.26)

Specifies a market, the publishing status of the product in that market, and supply details for that market. It is repeatable to allow description of multiple markets.

P.24 Market

Specifies the geographical market in which a product is distributed and any applicable sales restrictions.

P.25 Market Publishing Detail

Carries information about the publishing status of a product within a specific market. Information that can be carried includes the publisher representative, agent information, website, product contact information, publishing date (if the date is specific to a particular market), promotion campaign information, print run, copies sold in a previous version, and book club information.

P.26 Supply Detail

Carries information about availability and price for a specified market. This is a complex group and there are many optional composites but, if needed, it allows expression of variations in availability and price related to specific suppliers, prices applicable to different types of customers and prices in different currencies, for example.

Changes in ONIX 3.0

A complete introduction to ONIX 3.0 can be found in the ONIX *Specification* and *Implementation and Best Practice Guide*, available from the EDItEUR website. Guidelines for ONIX 3.0 changes relating to digital products are available in the EDItEUR document *How to Describe Digital Products in ONIX 3.0* and are also covered in Chapter 6 of this Handbook.

Following are brief descriptions of the ten key areas of change between ONIX 2.1 and ONIX 3.0.

1. **Removal of redundant elements**
Elements marked as deprecated in the latest ONIX 2.1 revision are deleted along with elements made redundant by new features in ONIX 3.0.

2. **Description of digital elements**
Handling of digital products is significantly revised to better meet current descriptive and business needs for these products.

3. **Handling of multi-item products, series, and sets**
Problems with earlier versions identified by ONIX users are addressed with this new approach, using `<Collection>` instead of `<Series>` or `<Set>`.

4. **Publishers' marketing collateral**
New data element groups are added to cover the greater variety of marketing collateral made available by publishers and aggregators.

5. **Sales and distribution in international markets**
The elements included allow clear and accurate description of product status.

6. **Products related to a single work**
Products can be related to a parent work to identify different editions of the same text or "work." ONIX 2.1 could specify the ISTC for the work described in the product record. ONIX 3.0 can specify the ISTC for any predecessor work (the original language version of a work in translation, for example) or a work derived from the product being described.

7. **Multilingual metadata**
Textual metadata can be provided in multiple languages within a single record — providing both a Spanish and English description of the same book, for example.

8. **Blocked records for more efficient updating**
Updates can be sent in applicable "blocks" without sending a complete record replacement. This significantly reduces the amount of data that needs to be sent.

9. New schema options
ONIX for Books XML schema definition and the codelists are available in the ISO standard RNG schema as well as W3C DTD and XSD schema languages.

10. Implementation and best practice guide
Extensive guidance on implementation and best practices is now available and is intended to act as a global benchmark and to help ensure global interoperability.

ONIX Tools and Documentation

ONIX is an open standard, maintained by the international standards organization EDItEUR, and there is no cost for using it. ONIX implementation tools and documentation are available for download free of charge from the EDItEUR website. Materials for each release include the following:

- XML Document Type Definition (DTD) and/or Schema
- Documentation specifying the data content of a standard ONIX message or data file
- XML tools, such as the tagname converter
- Documents providing guidance on how to implement ONIX

Other Schemes

MARC 21

As discussed in Chapter 2, MARC (MAchine Readable Cataloging) was developed in the late 1960s as a way to store and share library cataloging record in electronic format. The most commonly implemented version, MARC 21, was introduced in 1997.

This *Handbook* provides only a very general overview of MARC in its role as a widely used international metadata standard and as it relates to interoperability between publishing industry metadata and library metadata. In-depth information on MARC 21 is available from the Library of Congress website and further resources are provided in the *Handbook's* **Bibliography and References** section.

The structure of MARC records is an implementation of national and international standards such as *Information Interchange Format* (ANSI Z39.2) and *Format for Information Exchange* (ISO 2709).

The content of MARC records is defined outside of the format by standards such as the Anglo-American Cataloging rules, discussed Chapter 3.

MARC format is a set of codes and content designators to encode machine-readable records. Although "coded" to allow machine-to-machine communication, MARC does not utilize controlled vocabulary or code lists that refer to and translate to textual statements nearly as extensively as ONIX. As a result, a large part of the MARC record is actual text and can't be interpreted as accurately and consistently in an automated way.

Following are the major tags and field names of a MARC record. Many will be familiar as common elements used to describe books. Many also have more-or-less direct equivalents in ONIX.

1XX	Main Entry (Either a Name or a Uniform Title)
20X-24X	Title and Title-Related Fields
25X-28X	Edition and Imprint
3XX	Physical Description
4XX	Series
5XX	Notes
6XX	Subjects
70X-75X	Added Entries (Additional contributors, titles, etc.)
76X-78X	Linking Entries (Links to other editions, forms, original language version, translations, etc.)
8XX	Series Added Entries, and other general information

The specialized nature of the MARC record and MARC-based systems limits its use outside of the library environment. In 2002, the Library of Congress introduced the MARC-XML schema as an alternative structure, allowing better use of MARC by web services. However, the content and format of MARC still create barriers to interoperability.

OCLC, the Library of Congress, EDItEUR, and others have worked toward the ability to crosswalk between ONIX and MARC, allowing metadata to be more easily shared between libraries and the trade supply chain. But the current landscape still encourages tremendous duplication of effort in metadata creation and inhibits sharing metadata for the same titles.

In October 2011, the Library of Congress announced a commitment to work toward "A Bibliographic Framework for the Digital Age." Quoting the Library's *Working Group for the Future of Bibliographic Control,* the announcement recognized that "MARC is based on forty-year-old techniques for data management and is out of step with programming styles of today."

As the library community moves toward 21st century solutions, library materials and metadata providers will continue respond to libraries' day-to-day need for bibliographic data in MARC format.

Dublin Core

Dublin Core grew out of 1995 meeting held at the library organization OCLC, located in Dublin, Ohio, to explore the creation of a core data set for describing Web-based resources. The standard originally included "Simple" and "Qualified" levels. The simple Dublin Core Metadata Element Set (DCMES) consists of fifteen elements. Qualified Dublin Core included additional elements – audience, provenance, and rightsHolder - as well as a group of qualifiers used to refine elements.

Since 2012, these two sets have been consolidated into the DCMI Metadata Terms as a single set. Following is the current Dublin Core set. The original fifteen "Simple" elements are in ***bold italics***.

- abstract
- accessRights
- accrualMethod
- accrualPeriodicity
- accrualPolicy
- alternative
- audience
- available
- bibliographicCitation
- conformsTo
- ***contributor***
- ***coverage***
- created
- ***creator***
- ***date***
- dateAccepted
- dateCopyrighted
- dateSubmitted
- ***description***
- educationLevel
- extent
- ***format***
- hasFormat
- hasPart
- hasVersion
- ***identifier***
- instructionalMethod
- isFormatOf
- isPartOf
- isReferencedBy
- isReplacedBy
- isRequiredBy
- issued
- ***language***
- license
- mediator
- medium
- modified
- provenance
- ***publisher***
- references
- ***relation***
- replaces
- requires
- ***rights***
- rightsHolder
- ***source***
- spatial
- ***subject***
- tableOfContents
- temporal
- ***title***
- ***type***
- valid

Among many other applications, the EPUB standard uses Dublin Core to express metadata within electronic publications. Chapter 9 provides more information about metadata as it is used within digital content files.

Schema.org

In 2011, Google, Yahoo!, Bing, and Yandex (a Russian search engine), began working together toward creating a common set of schemes for markup of structured data on websites. The goal was to help search engines understand websites better. This doesn't replace the structured metadata delivered in XML carriers such as ONIX, but rather helps search engines gain direct access to and better understanding of this metadata in the Web's HTML environment, resulting in richer search results.

. . . .

Standards for Subjects

Providing accurate and useful terminology to describe a book's subject and genre has been important for as long as books have existed. The earliest libraries physically grouped books by subject and included subject information in written catalogs.

In some ways this is even more important in an online search environment since subjects allow lists of books to be selected, sorted, and presented to readers as groups of titles organized by subject or genre. Subjects are at work when a user searches or browses by subject and behind the scenes via a website's algorithms designed to present titles of potential interest to readers.

This particular type of information organization, whether in physical shelving or in online search, only works well when subjects are presented consistently through use of controlled vocabularies. This means the person selecting a subject (or subjects) selects from a defined list of terms rather than making up keywords or phrases that might not be consistent across a large group of titles or properly indexed in bookseller or library systems.

Following are the major standards used by the book industry and libraries to describe a book's subject. The practical application of subjects (and keywords) is covered in Part 3, Chapter 8, **Search Engine Optimization, Keywords, and Subjects**.

Book industry standards include:

- **BISAC Subject Headings**
  BISAC Subject Headings are the North American standard for categorizing books based on topical content or genre. Updated yearly through input from a committee of industry experts, they are maintained by the Book Industry Study Group (BISG). Documentation specifying the data content of a standard ONIX message or data file.

- **Book Industry Communication (BIC) Standard Subject Categories**
  BIC Categories are the UK standard for categorizing books.

- **Thema Category Scheme**
  Thema is a new global subject classification system for books, which is gathering wide international participation. Thema aims to reduce the duplication of effort in maintaining and applying multiple national subject schemes and the need for mapping between schemes. It can be used along with existing schemes, such as BISAC and BIC, and may eventually replace them.

Library standards include:

- **Library of Congress Subject Headings (LCSH)**
  Actively maintained by the Library of Congress since 1898, Library of Congress Subject Headings

are used by national and international libraries to provide subject access to collections

- **Library of Congress Classification**
Developed in the late 19th and early 20th centuries to organize the Library of Congress collection, this classification system is widely adopted by other libraries, especially large academic libraries in the United States. It is also one of the most widely used classification systems in the world.

- **Dewey Decimal Classification (DDC)**
The DDC was first developed and published by Melvil Dewey in 1876. Now in its twenty-third major edition, it is maintained and licensed by OCLC, a global library cooperative. The DDC has been translated into more than 30 languages, and with adoption by libraries in more than 135 countries, is the world's most widely used library classification system.

Chapter 5: National and International Standards Organizations

Standards organizations are focused on the development, communication, administration, and continued revision of technical standards. The organizations are formed to address the needs of a broad group of adopters, or an entire industry, and usually address the need to govern the standard in a way that is independent of any individual commercial organization. Most standards are voluntary and are not mandated by law. "Formal standards" are those that have been approved by organizations charged by an industry or group with setting technical standards.

International Standards Organizations

International standards organizations develop standards that are used across countries and geographic boundaries, with membership and representation from multiple countries. The three largest and most established are the International Organization for Standardization (ISO), the International Electrotechnical Commission (IEC), and the International Telecommunication Union (ITU), all in existence for more than fifty years and all based in Geneva, Switzerland.

Formal standards organizations are essential to widespread adoption of new technologies, especially through their role in the development and support of standards that facilitate interoperability across products and determine a baseline for continued research and product development. When a standard is developed, vetted, approved, published, and supported by an international standards organization, the industry has a high degree of confidence that adoption of that standard will result in products and processes that work in multiple environments and markets.

National Standards Organizations

Most countries have a single recognized national standards organization that participates in ISO. The American National Standards Institute (ANSI) plays this role in the U.S., the British Standards Institution (BSI) in the UK, and the Standards Council of Canada (SCC) in Canada.

A national standards organization may not develop standards itself but rather oversee and accredit the procedures of standards developing groups. For example, multiple U.S. organizations contribute to standards ultimately approved and published by ANSI. For the publishing industry, libraries, and developers of information-based software, products and services, NISO (National Information Standards Organization) plays the biggest role in the development and support of relevant industry standards.

ISO and NISO

ISO

The organization known today as ISO began in 1926 as the International Federation of the National Standardizing Organizations (ISA), and was strongly focused on mechanical engineering. After WWII, it was reorganized under the current name.

ISO is a voluntary organization made up of national standards bodies from 164 countries. The organization has published over 19,000 International Standards covering most aspects of technology and manufacturing. Based in Geneva, Switzerland, ISO has over 150 full-time employees.

NISO

NISO is a member of and is accredited by the United States ISO representative organization, ANSI. NISO was founded in 1939, was incorporated in 1983, and assumed its current name in 1984. Its mission statement is as follows:

> NISO fosters the development and maintenance of standards that facilitate the creation, persistent management, and effective interchange of information so that it can be trusted for use in research and learning.

The International ISBN Agency and National ISBN Registration Agencies

The International ISBN Agency

Located in the UK and managed by EDItEUR, the main functions of the International ISBN Agency as defined on their website are:

- To promote, coordinate and supervise the world-wide use of the ISBN system
- To approve the definition and structure of group agencies
- To allocate group identifiers to group agencies
- To advise on the establishment and functioning of group agencies
- To advise group agencies on the allocation of international publisher identifiers
- To publish the assigned group numbers and publishers' prefixes

The ISBN Agency Board governs the organization. The Board meets twice a year and consists of eight elected members and five ex officio members.

The International ISBN Agency does not issue ISBNs except to multi-national non-government organizations (NGOs). Publishers apply for ISBNs through National Registry Agencies.

National ISBN Registration Agencies

For the purposes of ISBN registration, a publisher is the entity responsible for initiating the production of a publication. This can be an individual, a group, a company, or an organization.

The location of publisher operations determines which agency will supply the publisher's ISBNs. If the organization has more than one site, ISBN registration is based on the location of company headquarters. ISBN registry is not based on location(s) of publication printing, manufacturing, marketing, or distribution or on language of publication.

The ISBN Registration Agency for the U.S. is Bowker Identifier Services, a division of R. R. Bowker. The agency for the UK is Nielsen UK ISBN Agency. The Canadian ISBN Service System, a division of Library and Archives Canada, issues ISBNs in that country.

The International ISBN Agency does not determine the cost of ISBNs. Each national registration agency determines the fee structure for its services — the cost of ISBN assignment and the details of the process involved are different for each agency. Some agencies, such as the Canadian ISBN Service System, may issue ISBNs free of charge.

ISBN registration requires the publisher to provide metadata about the publication. The type and format of required metadata is established by the International ISBN Agency in coordination with the national agencies. Providing this metadata may also result in the addition of publication information to industry databases maintained by the registration agencies. For Bowker and Nielsen, these databases drive products and services independent of ISBN registration functions. Both Bowker and Nielsen are also data aggregators, selling products and services based on aggregated book data. In the U.S., ISBN registration ensures the publication will be listed in Bowker's *Books in Print®* and, in the UK, in Nielsen BookData. The nature of these products and services is described in the **Data Aggregators** section of Chapter 2.

Registration for Other Identifiers

Bowker and Nielsen also serve as registration agencies for the SAN (Standard Address Number) and the ISTC (International Standard Text Code) described in Chapter 4.

In addition, Bowker is involved in the ISNI (International Standard Name Identifier) for identification of public identities (such as author names), and may become an ISNI registration agency.

The *National ISBN Agencies and Identifier Services* chart provides an overview of the agencies and their services.

National ISBN Agencies & Identifier Services

UNITED STATES	CANADA (English Language Books)	UNITED KINGDOM
ISBN – International Standard Book Number		
Bowker Identifier Services	The Canadian ISBN Service System *Library and Archives Canada*	Nielsen UK ISBN Agency
SAN – Standard Address Number		
Bowker Identifier Services	Assigned by the U.S. SAN Agency. **(Bowker Identifier Service)**	Nielsen SAN Agency
ISSN – International Standard Serial Number		
U.S. ISSN Center *Library of Congress*	ISSN Canada *Library and Archives Canada*	ISSN UK Centre *British Library*
ISTC – International Standard Text Number		
Bowker Identifier Services ISTC	No agency yet for English language publications. BTLF is the agency for French-language publications.	Nielsen ISTC Agency
LCCN – Library of Congress Control Number		
Preassigned Control Number Program *Library of Congress*	n/a	n/a

EDItEUR and the ONIX Standard

EDItEUR was established in 1994, initially to coordinate the development of electronic commerce standards for books and serials, and is responsible for the implementation and maintenance of ecommerce message formats for these sectors. The two generations of e-commerce message standards maintained by EDItEUR are EDIFACT, the UN-ECE (United Nations Economic Commission for Europe) standard for international trading communication (somewhat similar to the X12 standards maintained by BISG for use in North America), and EDitX, a modern family of XML message formats developed by EDItEUR and tailored to individual book trade applications.

EDItEUR is an international not-for-profit membership organization that provides a center of expertise for identifier and metadata standards for its members and on behalf of the book and journal industry as a whole. It has around 100 members from twenty-one countries, including Australia, Canada, China, Japan, United States, and most European countries. Membership is open to any organization with an interest in e-commerce for books and serials or related identification and metadata standards. Further membership details can be found on the EDItEUR website.

EDItEUR administers the ONIX (ONline Information eXchange) family of standards, including ONIX for Books, ONIX for Serials, and ONIX for Publication Licenses. All these standards are free of charge to download and use, and are not limited to members. The organization also plays a role in the administration and registration of identifiers, including management of the International ISBN Agency and a more limited support role for the International ISTC Agency.

First published in 2000 and currently in Version 3.0.2, The ONIX for Books Product Information Message is the international standard for representation and communication of book industry information in electronic form. The American Association of Publishers (AAP) was critical to the initial development of ONIX. ONIX 1.0 was published in January 2000, with the assistance of Book Industry Communication (BIC) and EDItEUR. EDItEUR now develops, maintains and promotes the standard with the assistance of BIC and the Book Industry Study Group (BISG), and under the guidance of an International Steering Committee that includes representation from BIC, BISG, and other national user groups in Australia, Belgium, Canada, China, Egypt, Finland, France, Germany, Italy, Japan, Korea, The Netherlands, Norway, Russia, Spain, and Sweden. National groups can be set up in any country with a significant number of ONIX implementers, and these groups can each be represented on the International Steering Committee. The national groups have a key governance role in ensuring that the standard is suitable for global use, and that it meets evolving business requirements.

The *ONIX Users and Services Directory* on the EDItEUR website lists a small selection of the organizations using ONIX. BISG also maintains an *ONIX Users Directory* that includes ONIX senders, receivers, and technical service providers.

Part 3: Essential Metadata Elements

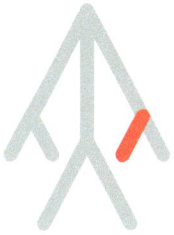

Metadata is used in almost every aspect of publishing and should meet the needs of the entire publishing organization (acquisitions, editorial, marketing, production, etc.), as well as the needs of booksellers, other trading partners, and readers. Effective metadata supports all publishing and bookselling activities.

The necessary minimum set of data elements ultimately depends on the publisher's business requirements and the requirements of the publisher's supply chain partners rather than on a centrally defined set. However, publishing industry organizations develop and communicate metadata best practices recommendations, including identification of the metadata elements that are important in the publisher supply chain. Recipients of publisher metadata often have core requirements, including the presence of a specific set of metadata elements. Industry-defined recommended best practices are covered in Part 4. The elements described here are consistent with those recommended in publishing industry best practices documentation.

This section looks at important metadata elements as they relate to overall bookselling needs, exploring why they're important and how they support publishing and bookselling activities. The focus here is on the elements themselves rather than on metadata carriers such as ONIX.

Chapter 6: Essential Elements for All Books

Metadata is used in almost every aspect of publishing.

- Acquisition
- Rights
- Editorial
- Production
- Marketing
- Distribution
- Merchandising
- Search
- Discovery
- Selection
- Ordering
- Sales transactions
- Sales tracking
- Business intelligence

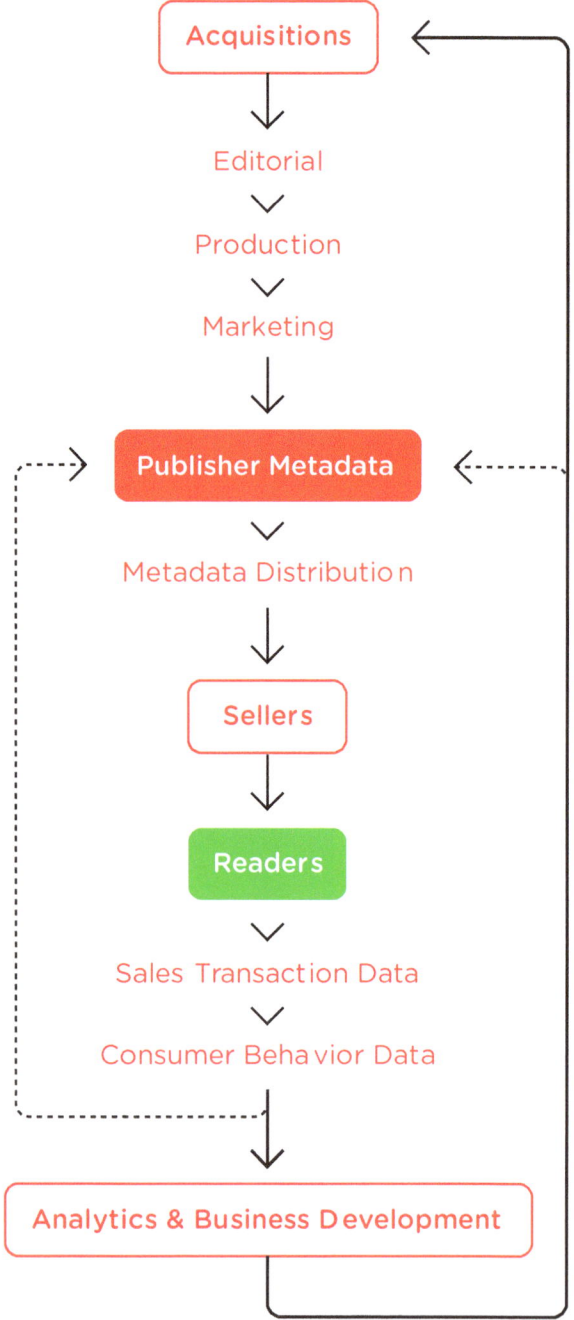

Ideally, each publisher would maintain one comprehensive database that contains all the data needed for these functions and that works for all users — publisher staff, sales channels, trading partners, and readers. Even when this isn't the case, metadata distributed into the marketplace must meet the basic needs of 21st century online bookselling and e-commerce.

Data that works supports the functions and user needs above and covers three basic areas: content description, product description, and commerce needs.

Metadata for Content Description

Good description is at the heart of successful online selling for any product. Whether you're selling shoes, refrigerators, or books, the metadata describing the product stands in for the physical item and must, at the very least, accurately express the nature and qualities of what is being sold. In an online selling environment, and especially for digital books with no physical counterpart, metadata IS the user experience and provides the basis purchasing decisions.

The following elements are the basic building blocks for describing the content of a book. They refer to the work itself rather than how it is packaged (hardcover, paperback, or digital, for example) and most will apply to any version of the book that has the same content. When a publisher issues the same content in multiple formats, it's very important that content description is consistent across the versions. Note that some elements listed, such as series and edition, are essential only when applicable to the book.

- **Title**
- **Subtitle** (when applicable)
- **Contributor(s)**
- **Edition** (when applicable)
- **Series** (when applicable)
- **Language of content**
- **Intended audience**
- **Age level** (for juvenile and young adult titles)
- **Description**
- **Subject(s)**

It's also important to provide information about other products related to the content described.

- **Related Products** - This metadata element is used to indicate a new edition that supersedes older one; multiple versions of products with the same content, or content that's part of a multi-part product.

Use of Metadata for Content Description in Website Display

hachettebookgroup.com

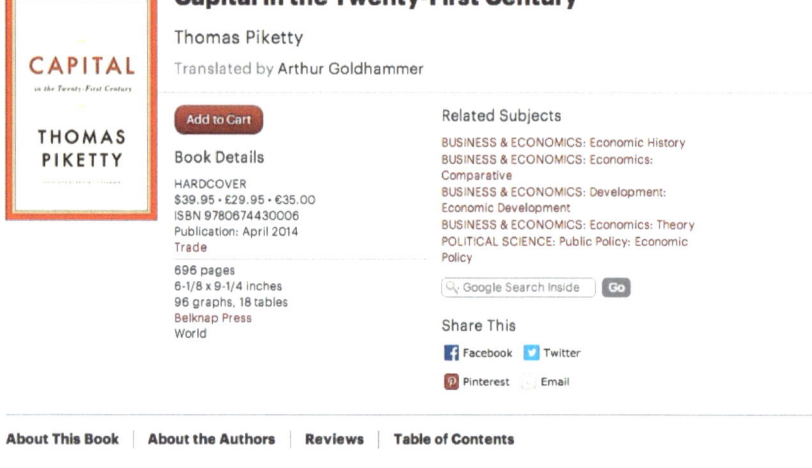

hachettebookgroup.com

Metadata for Product Description

Metadata must also communicate certain things about the nature of the particular product type, or version, of the content. A book can have the same title, author, edition, description, language, and subjects, but the fact that it's in audio, digital, hardcover, or paperback format matters to the reader, the seller, and the publisher.

Publishers must maintain accurate product information to effectively track sales and marketing information associated with particular formats. For example, it matters that a book enjoys strong sales in print but weak sales in the audio version. This has implications for marketing strategy, analysis of consumer behavior, and business intelligence regarding the effectiveness of various types of content in each available format.

Complete and accurate product information is crucial for resellers as well. For example, wholesalers use information about weight, dimensions, and number of pieces to plan inventory space and anticipate shipping charges for physical items.

- **ISBN**
- **Cover image**
- **Publisher and Imprint**
- **Product form** (format, binding, packaging)
- **Extent** (page count, file size)
- **Physical dimensions and Weight** (for physical products)
- **Number of pieces** (When applicable for physical products)
- **DRM/Usage constraints** (for digital products)
- **Software/Hardware requirements** (when applicable)

The following products are all versions of the same basic content in different formats. Many of the elements listed above may be different for different formats, and some won't be applicable to all, based on whether the format is digital, print, or audio.

Use of Metadata for Product Description in Website Display

Hardcover

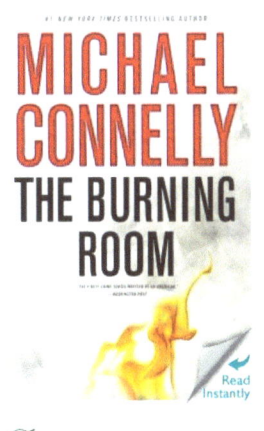

Use of Metadata for Product Description in Website Display

Ebook

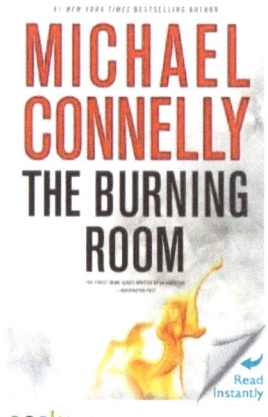

barnesandnoble.com

The Burning Room (Harry Bosch Series #19) [NOOK Book]
by Michael Connelly

★★★★ (121)   Add to List +   Pin it   g+1 1   Like Share

Overview - In the new thriller from #1 New York Times bestselling author Michael Connelly, Detective Harry Bosch and his rookie partner investigate a cold case that gets very hot... very fast. In the LAPD's Open-Unsolved Unit, not many murder victims die a decade after the crime. So when a man succumbs to complications from being shot by a stray bullet ten years earlier, Bosch catches a case in which the body is still fresh, but any other clues are ... See more details below

Product Details
ISBN-13: 9780316225922
Publisher: Little, Brown and Company
Publication date: 11/3/2014
Series: Harry Bosch Series , #19
Sold by: Hachette Digital, Inc.
Format: eBook
Sales rank: 13
File size: 2 MB

Audiobook

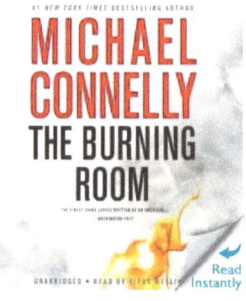

Sale • Bestselling Audio Books Up to 40% Off

barnesandnoble.com

The Burning Room (Harry Bosch Series #19)
by Michael Connelly, Titus Welliver (Read by)

★★★★ (121)   Add to List +   Pin it   g+1 0   Like Share

Overview - The new thriller from #1 *New York Times* bestselling author Michael Connelly follows Detective Harry Bosch and his new partner as they investigate a recent murder where the trigger was pulled nine years earlier. In the LAPD's Open-Unsolved Unit, not many murder victims die almost a decade after the crime. So when a man succumbs to complications from being shot by a stray bullet nine years earlier, Bosch catches a case in which the body is still ... See more details below

Product Details
ISBN-13: 9781619694262
Publisher: Hachette Audio
Publication date: 11/3/2014
Series: Harry Bosch Series , #19
Format: CD
Edition description: Unabridged
Pages: 8
Sales rank: 14,847
Product dimensions: 5.25 (w) x 5.75 (h) x 1.50 (d)

Metadata for Commerce

Of course consumers, publishers, and booksellers all care about the price, but for publishers and resellers, there are many additional metadata needs connected to buying and selling. The elements below drive how, when, at what price, and, in the case of territorial rights, even if books can be bought and sold. Many of these elements aren't visible to the consumer but they drive business decisions behind the scenes.

- Price
- Bar Code (for physical products)
- Publication date
- Strict-on-sale date (if applicable)
- Status code
- Product availability code
- Publisher's proprietary discount
- Distributor/Vendor of record
- Country of manufacture (for physical products)
- Territorial rights
- Case pack/Carton quantity (for physical products)
- Return code (if applicable)

Examples

Publishers are expected to send their selling partners a **Status code** along with a **Publication date**. Status codes provide the seller with information about:

- When a book has been published and is available for delivery
- When a book is forthcoming
- When a book was previously announced as forthcoming, but has been cancelled
- When a book that was previously available is no longer available from that publisher or vendor

In an online bookstore web display, the consumer will see information about forthcoming books in a way similar to the following example.

If a book also has a **Strict-on-sale date**, the bookseller is not to deliver the book to the customer until the exact day/month/year specified.

Elements such as **Territorial rights** aren't visible to the consumer but drive where books may be legally bought and sold.

Use of Metadata for Commerce in Website Display

A Banquet of Consequences: A Lynley Novel (Inspector Lynley Book 19) by Elizabeth George (Oct 6, 2015)

amazon.com

Formats	Price	New	Used
Kindle Edition Available for Pre-order	$14.99		
Hardcover Available for Pre-order FREE Shipping on orders over $35 and 1 more promotion	$29.95 $21.74 ✓Prime		

Other Formats: Audio CD

Part 3: Essential Metadata Elements   *Chapter 6: Essential Elements for All Books*

Chapter 7: Enhancing Metadata to Stand Out in the Marketplace

Including essential metadata facilitates efficient buying and selling processes and provides the basics needed for search and discovery in web-based environments. However, additional information can be a differentiating factor in exposing titles and in user selection. Enhanced and evaluative information, such as reviews, author information and interviews, excerpts, and videos enrich the user's experience in ways that aren't possible in a printed book. The addition of important metadata over the life of the title contributes to continued interest and sales long after book launch.

Some valuable information is not available prepublication or even at the initial publication date. The title will continue to be reviewed after publication and book awards will be announced. New information about authors, including author awards and other distinctions, should be added as appropriate. Promotional information, media attention, and author interviews can be added as well.

Following are metadata enhancements that make a difference.

- Excerpts, previews, and sample chapters
- Awards
- Reviews
- Contributor biographies, interviews, and touring schedules
- Video content (trailers, for example)
- Tables of contents
- Digital images in addition to the cover image

Use of Metadata Enhancements in Website Display

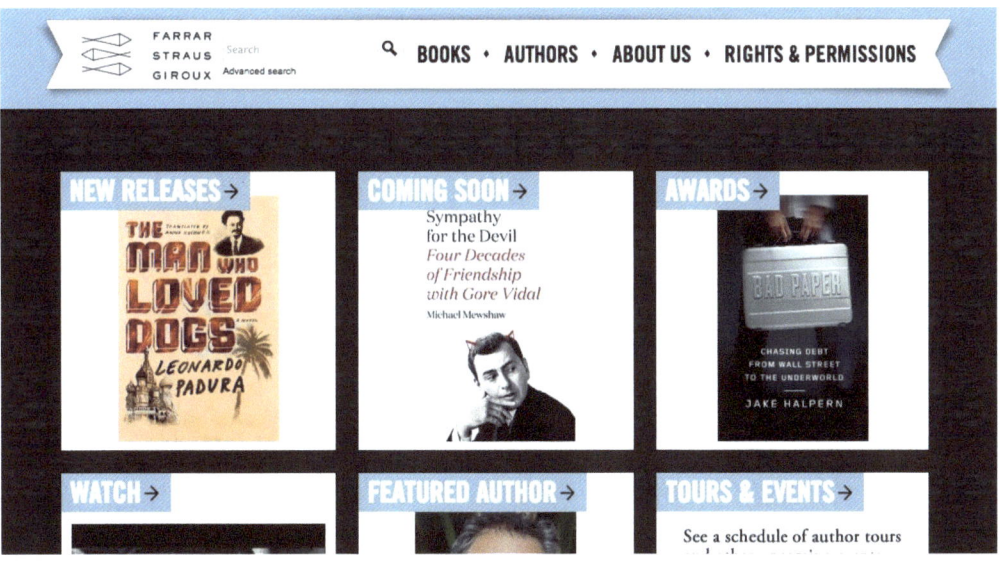

macmillan.com/fsg

Use of Metadata Enhancements in Website Display

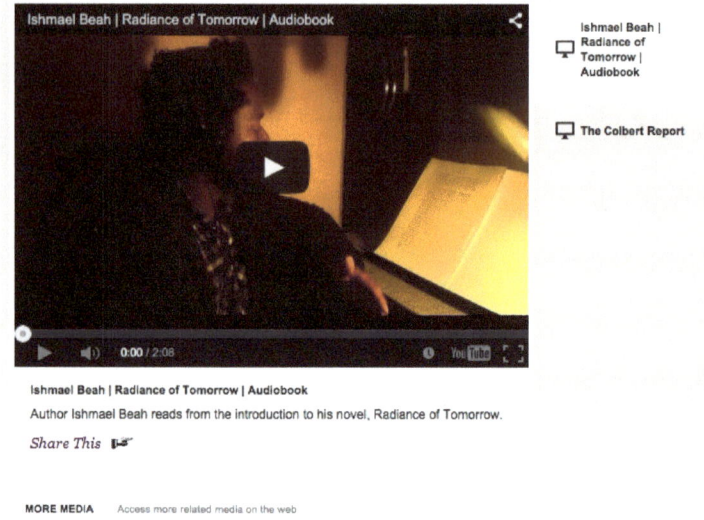

hachettebookgroup.com

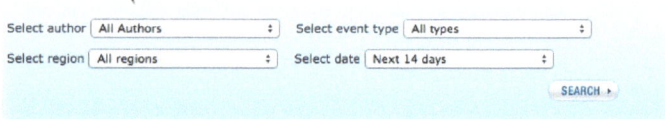

macmillan.com/fsg

macmillan.com/fsg

Chapter 8: Search Engine Optimization, Keywords, and Subjects

Metadata is central to search engine optimization (SEO) for all books that are sold online, both print and digital. Search engines rank and display search results based on algorithms designed to determine which sites and/or product pages are most relevant to the user's search. Bookseller search engines also use algorithms to present users with title recommendations that don't derive from a specific search. Taking full advantage of metadata options for product description helps ensure results that are truly relevant to readers and keeps readers engaged with the information they find.

SEO and Keywords

When publishers and self-published authors think about search engine optimization, they often pay a lot of attention to the selection of keywords. Early on there were all sorts of attempts to game the keyword system to make it more likely to be found via search engines. The common thinking today is that good descriptive metadata (as opposed to keyword stuffing and other tricks that are now detected and punished by search engines) is also the best way to optimize for search.

Attention to keywords and phrases is still important, but marketing content should not be written just around keywords or phrases, but with the intended audience in mind, considering the most compelling way to describe the book. Keywords that duplicate metadata found elsewhere in the product record are next to useless since those words and phrases are already present and used in search.

The industry still struggles to understand how keywords work in a real search environment and there has been a lack of industry best practices and recommendations for their use. Many major metadata receivers (wholesalers, distributors, and retailers) don't even use them because they've found them to be redundant, poorly selected, and even misleading. Help is here. The Book Industry Study Group (BISG) organized a Keywords Working Group in 2013 and published *Best Practices for Keywords in Metadata: Guide for North American Data Senders and Receivers* in 2014. The guide is available for download at no charge from BISG.

Keywords and BISAC Subject Headings

Keywords are not a substitute for controlled subject vocabularies such as BISAC Subject Headings. These vocabularies expressing subject and genre drive the way in which bookseller websites are organized and work behind the scenes to expose relevant lists of titles to readers. Most major book vendors require that publisher data feeds contain at least one BISAC Subject Heading for each title.

Booksellers may display their own lists of subject terms on their websites that are slightly different from the BISAC vocabulary. In these cases, publishers are still sending BISAC codes that the vendor then maps to their preferred terminology. Following are examples of how BISACs are used to organize title display and to lead readers to other books with similar subjects or genres.

macmillan.com/fsg

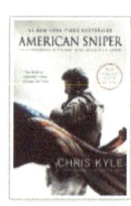
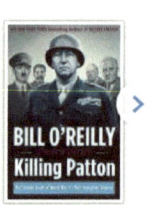

macmillan.com/fsg

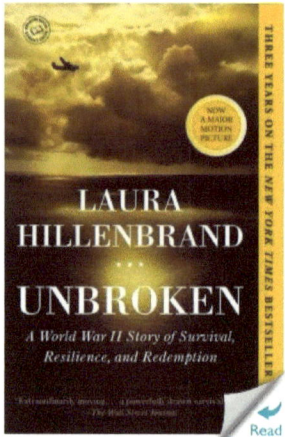

The entire list of BISAC Subject Headings is available on the BISG website, along with guidance for their use (see the **Bibliography and References** section), but here are a few general rules.

- Never use a general BISAC when a more specific one is appropriate and available. Using a general term does not bring a book to a wider audience. Instead the book is lost in a sea of books that are categorized too generally. These books are unlikely to be exposed through search algorithms that identify and display similar titles to readers.
- Don't send a general term along with a more specific term that's in the same subject area. Most vendors will simply drop the general term. For example, don't send both FICTION-GENERAL and FICTION-MYSTERY for the same title.
- Don't combine Juvenile and Adult Subject Headings. The subjects chosen should match the intended audience chosen. If juvenile or young adult is chosen as intended audience, juvenile subjects should be used.

Choose subjects carefully as they are extremely valuable in search. Use the same principles discussed above when choosing from a list of subjects offered by self-publishing platforms. There is no need to duplicate words or phrases in BISAC Subject Headings (or other controlled lists of subject terms) in a keyword list. Use keywords to express aspects of the book and ways users might search that can't be expressed in Subject Headings or other metadata elements.

Bookseller Website Search Engines

Searches on proprietary search engines for consumer sites (Amazon, Barnes & Noble, and publisher websites, for example) are directed specifically at the seller's database of information about books. Publishers contribute directly to this metadata through data feeds to sellers.

Including the essential metadata elements strongly contributes to search engine optimization, and enhancements add even more search result potential. Keywords may be indexed for search, but as mentioned earlier, many major bookseller sites do not expose them to consumers and may discard them entirely to protect database integrity and quality. Use of keywords such as "bestseller" and keywords or phrases consisting of the names of other titles that the publisher or author deems aimed at their intended audience (including the term "Harry Potter" with the metadata for an unrelated juvenile fantasy title, for example) contributes to sellers' distrust of keywords and the decision not to use them.

General Search Engines

Major search engines (Google, Yahoo, Bing, and others) search the entire web, including bookselling sites. It's not possible to control search engine algorithms or what Amazon does to optimize retrieval of their site by general search engines, but publishers can make sure that metadata distributed to all trading partners is as rich as possible. Sales ranking and other factors not directly related to book metadata certainly play a big part, but so do metadata completeness and quality. While there's no guarantee that complete metadata will result in a book's discovery, the absence of metadata will definitely guarantee its obscurity.

Chapter 9: Optimizing Product Metadata for Digital Publishing

The Essential Elements

Most metadata elements considered essential for bookselling apply equally to print and digital formats. The elements describing the content of a work should be complete and consistent (virtually identical) for all versions a book; elements for describing the product should match the product itself, clearly defining it as an unique sellable item; metadata supporting commerce must include all the information needed to effectively buy and sell a product across multiple booksellers. Following is a recap of metadata elements that are relevant to ebooks. The elements specific to physical products have been eliminated from the list.

Content Description

- Title
- Subtitle
- Contributor(s)
- Description
- Language of Content
- Subject(s)
- Intended Audience
- Age level (when the audience is juvenile or young adult)
- Edition
- Series

Product Description

- ISBN
- Cover Image
- Product Form
- Publisher/Imprint
- Extent
- Digital Rights Management (DRM) or Usage Constraints
- Software or Hardware Requirements

Commerce

- Price
- Territorial Rights
- Publication Date
- Strict-On-Sale Date (if applicable)
- Product Availability Code
- Publisher's Proprietary Discount
- Distributor/Vendor of Record

....

Ebooks and ISBNs

Assigning an ISBN to each digital format of a book is strongly recommended. The ability to consistently identify a book product across ever-increasing seller platforms remains important for effective bookselling. The proliferation of digital book formats, resulting in several product records for the same content, has some publishers concerned about the increased number of ISBNs needed to support multiple versions. As discussed in Chapter 5, in the United States and the United Kingdom, ISBNs cost money. This contributes to the dialog about additional ISBNs needed to identify digital versions, especially for smaller publishers.

Guidelines for assigning ISBNs to digital content are still evolving as the market itself grows and changes. In December 2011, the Book Industry Study Group (BISG) published the Policy Statement *Best Practices for Identifying Digital Products*. The document outlines cases in which a separate ISBN should be assigned due to difference in format, usage restrictions, and other variables. The document is consistent with the International ISBN Agency's (IIA) *Guidelines for the Assignment to E-books*, published November 25, 2010. As best practices continue to evolve based on market and technology factors, IIA, BISG, BNC, and BIC documentation will continue to provide valuable guidelines.

The increase in self-publishing platforms also contributes to the confusion around ISBN assignment. ISBNs may be assigned by third-party vendors as well as by publishers or self-published authors. Some self-publishing options don't require ISBNs for books created and distributed through digital publishing platforms, instead assigning their own unique internal identifiers. Chapter 11, *Metadata for Self-Publishers and Small Publishers*, discusses this in further detail. Publishers should discuss ISBN, and all metadata processes and issues, with their trading partners, including digital conversion and distribution services.

Expanded Options for Digital Content in ONIX 3.0

Fully describing specific digital formats and reading platforms requires metadata options beyond those needed for traditional books and metadata standards are evolving to meet those needs. Changes and additions in ONIX 3.0 are fully covered in Part 2, Chapter 4, but here's a reminder of 3.0 options allowing more flexibility in communicating Product Form and DRM information.

- New Product Form Codes to indicate that the product is digital and specify the delivery method
- New Product Form Detail and Product Form Feature elements and codes to specify digital formats and file types
- The ability to specify a Primary Content Type, including values such as "readable text," "audio book," and "music recording"
- Better coverage of DRM and usage constraints

Chapter 10: **Metadata in Digital Content Files**

This book is primarily about product metadata for books. The information included in product metadata files (consisting of individual product records) is sent separately from digital content files, and often well in advance of publication. Product metadata can also be updated throughout the life of a title.

Publishing in digital formats also provides ways to embed metadata into the actual ebook files. The metadata is carried along with the content of the book. This chapter explores the differences in how each type of metadata is used and the importance of taking advantage of both ways to provide metadata.

Uses of Metadata in Digital Content Files

Metadata that is embedded and carried in a digital content file serves several purposes. First, metadata tells the reading device what it has and what to do with it. It provides information such as file format and version, file creation date, text directionality (left-to-right or right-to-left), text reading order, information about how to display the cover, etc. This type of metadata ensures that a book will display properly on a reading device.

Ebook files also contain content and product information such as identifier, title, author, subject, extent, and other elements. This metadata is used to populate the "bookshelves" seen on reading platforms and devices. The metadata is viewed and used by readers to locate, organize, and select titles from their digital libraries. E-readers may differ in which metadata elements are displayed and in how they are displayed.

Digital file-level metadata is not a substitute for the product metadata that drives much of our book shopping experience, and it can't be updated without providing a new ebook file. However, publishers should make sure that basic metadata elements in digital book files are consistent with those in product metadata.

Taking responsibility for this metadata means that publishers should avoid relying on the default or limited metadata options sometimes provided by conversion or distribution services. As a rule, always add as much metadata as possible into the source file before conversion and work with digital service vendors to ensure source file metadata is handled correctly for effective use in reading devices.

Although not all reading devices currently display all available metadata options, publishers should take full advantage of available options, as there is great potential for new uses of this metadata in the future. Adding it to content now positions publishers to leverage it later.

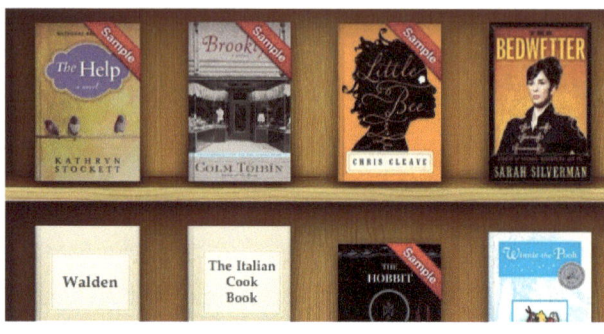

Metadata in the EPUB File Format

EPUB is the free, open standard maintained by the International Digital Publishing Forum (IDPF). Google Play, iBooks, NOOK® and many other reading systems work with EPUB documents. EPUB 3.0.1 is the most recent version of the standard, but some publishers and reading systems haven't implemented EPUB 3 yet and continue use of version 2.0.1.

Minimum required elements for EPUB 2.0.1 are title, language, and identifier. EPUB 3 requires the same three elements but also allows publishers to include many more data elements, including more identifiers and additional versions of the title. It also provides the ability to specify the metadata scheme defining the elements, such as MARC 21 or ONIX 3.0.

The following metadata components can be included in EPUB 2.0.1 and EPUB 3 files. Elements bolded are recommended for inclusion in every ebook file.

- **Title**
- **Creator**
- **Identifier/ISBN**
- **Language**
- **File name**
- **Type**
- **Format**
- Publisher
- Description
- Reviews
- Copyright
- Publication date
- Contributor
- Subject(s)
- Coverage (Localization)
- Source
- Relation
- Rights

EPUB 3 allows a much richer set of metadata elements. Almost any metadata element you can think of can be carried in EPUB 3. But publishers should carefully consider which metadata elements will permanently apply to the publication and are not subject to market changes. Metadata such as pricing and sales or territorial rights are best maintained outside of EPUB 3 metadata. It's also important to be aware that many metadata receivers will need to adapt their systems to accept this type of metadata before the full potential of EPUB 3 can be realized.

EPUB 3 allows metadata to be associated not only at the file level (metadata referring to the entire content package) but also at the component or element levels of the file down to the paragraph level. This opens up many options for rich metadata that can be attached to the actual content. It's also possible to include "external" product data, such as an ONIX file or a MARC record, within the EPUB 3 package, or to point to the external file through a link.

Many EPUB 3 features are implemented in major reading systems including iBooks, Kobo, CourseSmart, and VitalSouce. To reach its full potential as a carrier of both content and metadata, EPUB 3 must be broadly implemented by publishers and reading systems.

EPUB 3 is an ISO technical standard. Many publishing industry organizations, including the Association of

American Publishers (AAP), the Book Industry Study Group (BISG), EDItEUR, and the Readium Foundations, support EPUB 3 as the global standard format for ebooks. In October 2013, the AAP published the EPUB 3 Implementation White Paper. This document was developed as part of cross-industry project to advance the implementation of the EPUB 3 standard among publishers and reading systems.

If in the future, EPUB 3 is broadly implemented and fully supported by both publishers and data receivers, including both types of metadata in one package could reduce some of the current issues that can result from multiple data streams for different formats of the same work.

More information on EPUB 3 is provided in the **Bibliography and References** section.

Metadata in Proprietary Digital Formats

Although EPUB is the industry standard, some vendors make changes to the standard to create their own proprietary file format specifications. Amazon's KF8 (Kindle Format 8) is one example of a format that's different from the standard, making these files less interchangeable and adaptable.

These changes may give the individual sellers a competitive advantage and contribute to the user experience on their own devices, but they dilute the very meaning of an industry standard.

Chapter 11: Metadata for Self-Publishers and Small Publishers

Until fairly recently, the cost of publishing and distributing books was prohibitive for authors and small publishers. Publisher supply chain activities such as printing, marketing, advertising, distributing, and bookselling were optimized to create efficiencies for the major players. Direct-to-consumer bookselling websites and the rise of cost-effective digital publishing disrupted many of those activities. Although there are more options for authors and small publishers now, making sense of them can be confusing. This chapter provides guidance in using them wisely to compete in the marketplace.

Increasing consumer expectation of ebooks from traditional publishing houses and affordable options for self-publishing both contribute to changes in the publishing landscape. It's possible for an author to produce, publish, and sell a book outside of publishing industry production processes and established supply chain distribution channels. This also opens up new business models for small publishers, allowing them to reach the marketplace at a reasonable cost, even without the economies of scale enjoyed by large publishers.

But new platforms for self-publishing, many of which are tied to proprietary reading devices and digital formats, also operate on different business models and technology. Books published in this way remain outside many mainstream publishing options, including some of the metadata options described in this book. Self-published authors and small publishers producing books in this way must enter metadata manually and are limited to the metadata options provided in the platform's interface for creating and uploading ebooks.

When the publishing technology is tied to a specific device that is also sold by the vendor, selling on that vendor's website may be the only place the book (in that format) can be sold. If the author or publisher wants to make the book available to readers on other devices and to be sold on different sites, the process must be repeated on different platforms with different options for both content and metadata.

It's beyond the scope of this chapter to compare or recommend services based on metadata potential and all the others aspects of self-publishing services. The intention is to provide information for authors and publishers to consider when choosing how to publish digital content.

Identifiers: ISBN, Proprietary Identifier Systems, and Industry Databases

Many of the new self-publishing platforms allow books to be published and sold without an ISBN. This automatically places books published in this way outside of international publishing standards. The non-ISBN identifier assigned in the publishing process is proprietary to that bookseller and means nothing outside that particular vendor system.

This may also result in keeping these publications outside of industry databases of published titles, such as Bowker *Books in Print* in the U.S. These databases capture and distribute book metadata to the industry at large. A book may be published and available from one or more sellers but not listed in the national or international databases that strive to list all available titles. It isn't visible to any consumer, seller, or library using this tool to locate books.

ISBNs cost money in the U.S. and the decision on whether or not to obtain an ISBN when the seller doesn't require one remains with the author or publisher, but obtaining an ISBN does increase selling options and market visibility.

Obtaining an ISBN through ISBN Registration Agencies

For those publishing one title or a small number of titles, the ISBN registration process is manual. Bowker is the U.S. source for ISBNs. ISBNs are assigned through the Bowker Identifier Service and metadata submitted as part of the process is automatically added to the Bowker *Books in Print* database making the book visible and searchable for a large number of booksellers, libraries, and other organizations.

In response to the tremendous growth in self-publishing, Bowker also offers a service called Self Published Author, with packages that include conversion or production distribution and other services in addition to ISBN registration.

Bowker's selfpublishedauthor.com

Metadata in the ISBN Registration Process

Authors or publishers with less than 100 titles fall into the Bowker "self-publishing" category and title metadata is submitted manually. The ISBN registration tool for self-publishers offers the options of "Basic, Enhanced, and Enriched" metadata. These options include most of the elements discussed in this book. To fully leverage the opportunity to provide metadata to the broader marketplace, take advantage of all the options that apply to the publication.

Small publishers are defined as those with 100-499 titles per year. Metadata may be entered manually or may be supplied via ONIX, Excel, or text files and additional enhanced metadata elements are accepted.

ISBNs Provided by Self-Publishing Services

Many self-publishing services will provide an ISBN as part of their publishing packages. However, this means that they will be identified as the publisher of the book wherever the book is listed or sold. This may be fine for some authors or small publishers, but others will wish to publish under their own brand through the standard ISBN registration process. Most of these services allow a choice of providing an ISBN or using a vendor-provided ISBN.

Product Metadata Options in Self-Publishing Services

As discussed earlier, most self-publishing services provide an interface for manual entry of book metadata. The user is limited to the metadata options provided by the vendor. Although many of the essential metadata elements discussed in earlier sections of this book can be entered in most systems, the processes and options differ across platforms and may not allow the full range of metadata that is possible in a full ONIX record. If metadata self-entry tools don't include options for all the metadata elements desired, be sure to let the provider know of any concerns.

Make the most of what is available, even if all available fields aren't required. For example, Kindle Direct Publishing requires only the following metadata elements:

- Title
- Description
- Contributor(s)
- Language
- Publication rights
- Digital rights management

Complete all available and applicable metadata fields, even those that are not required. Be sure to provide a full and compelling description, a cover image, and the best and most specific of any subject and category selections available. Sometimes subject and category options are more limited in self-publishing platforms and may be different than those seen on the bookseller's main website category listings. The addition of multimedia elements such as trailers and author interviews aren't supported by some services.

Self-publishing and supporting services are evolving quickly, so perhaps with continued input from the community, product metadata options will become richer and more in line with those available for traditional publishing.

Digital File Metadata Options in Self-Publishing Services

Some metadata relating to the digital file itself is embedded as part of the production or conversion process. If possible, check with the vendor to see if there are options for providing metadata within the source file, if some of the product metadata provided as part of title setup is also included in the ebook file, and which metadata elements will be present in the final ebook file, including any that are system-generated.

This may be more difficult than it sounds. For example, the Amazon Kindle Direct Publishing site tells authors "not to worry" that product information provided during title setup doesn't appear when the file is previewed but that product metadata "will be included with the book file when it's published to the Kindle Store."

Ebook Distribution Options in Self-Publishing Services

Some self-publishing services create ebooks specifically for their own reading devices or apps and distribute only through their own bookselling websites. Examples include Amazon Kindle Direct and Kobo Writing Life. Publishing through a vendor's proprietary services doesn't prevent publishing and selling through other services. Just be aware that title set-up and ebook creation will required for other desired platforms and booksellers as well.

Some self-publishing services create files in multiple formats and distribute to multiple sellers. Bookbaby and Smashwords are two examples of the many available services. Files created in the EPUB format can be distributed to multiple sellers with reading platforms or devices that are built on EPUB, or a variation of EPUB. These include Apple's iBookstore and Barnes and Noble's NOOK bookstore.

Some services also offer conversion to formats required by reading platforms such as Amazon Kindle and Kobo and distribute to their bookstores. Distribution to Amazon is excluded by some so make sure to compare distribution options. Most also sell ebooks from their own bookstores.

New self-publishing services offering ebook creation with distribution to multiple sellers continue to emerge in direct response to the growth of and demand for one-stop digital publishing solutions. Some are new to the publishing industry and metadata options may be limited. Be aware of what's available in the title setup process, provide every metadata element allowed, and give feedback on any desired metadata elements that aren't offered.

Part 4: Metadata Best Practices and Certification Programs

Chapter 12: What Are Metadata Best Practices and How Are They Identified?

The purpose of establishing best practices in any industry is to encourage quality, promote standardization, and create efficiencies in business practices. In today's marketplace, the effective exchange of information is crucial. Metadata is a key asset in publishing and serves as the language of communication. It is the basis for business-to-business transactions and the foundation of consumer experience in online shopping environments.

Best Practices and Industry Standards

The terms "standards" and "best practices" are sometimes used interchangeably, but there are differences. For the purposes of this handbook, we'll define them as follows.

Standards

Standards are defined as a way of communicating or doing business that is approved and monitored by an authoritative agency or recognized body. ISBN is an example of a book industry standard. It is an ISO-approved standard administered by the International ISBN Agency. ONIX for Books and other members of the ONIX family are also recognized international standards and are administered by EDItEUR.

Except for those that are governmentally regulated, industry standards are generally voluntary. They are developed to create efficiencies and create interoperability between an industry's trading partners. Book industry organizations do not administer standards but they do actively support industry-wide adoption of standards to promote consistency and efficiency in the publisher supply chain. They also provide resources to assist in industry understanding and implementation of standards.

Best Practices

Best practices are recommendations and guidelines based on industry consensus and benchmarking. Some recommendations provide guidelines for the implementation and use of national and international standards and others communicate what the industry considers to be best business practices. Documentation published by industry organizations, such as the Book Industry Study Group's *Best Practices for Product Metadata*, offer accepted guidelines for the use of standards and for communicating book information in ways that have proven to work best for the book industry and for consumers.

The Role of Industry Organizations in Defining Best Practices

Trade organizations play a major role in promoting and publishing best practices for many industries. In Canada, this role is played by BookNet Canada, in the United States by the Book Industry Study Group (BISG), and in the United Kingdom by Book Industry Communication (BIC).

BISG, BookNet Canada, and BIC are membership organizations with representation from many parts of the publisher supply chain, and were created to support and encourage publishing industry relationships and the efficient exchange of information between trading partners. Best practices organizational committees and working groups are made up of representatives from the major segments of publishing and often work in coordination with other national and international standards organizations to provide input to standards development. They don't arbitrarily define industry standards or best practices, but build consensus through input from multiple publishing industry participants. They facilitate the development and communication of book industry standards and best practices, sponsor and publish research, and develop programs to support and encourage efficient and consistent exchange of information across publishing industry functions and players.

Information about key industry organization resources and publications is included in the **Bibliography and References** section.

Chapter 13: BISG's Best Practices for Product Metadata: Guide for North American Data Senders and Receivers

In 2013, The Book Industry Study Group (BISG), in coordination with BookNet Canada, released *Best Practices for Product Metadata: Guide for North American Data Senders and Receivers*, the first revision in BISG best practices documentation since 2005. This chapter focuses on that document.

History of BISG Best Practices Documentation

BISG first published *Product Metadata Best Practices for Senders* and *Product Metadata Best Practices for Receivers* in 2005. The documents were developed by the BISG Metadata Committee, comprised of representation from all parts of the publishing industry, including publishers, wholesalers, retailers, metadata aggregators, technology vendors, and libraries.

The Metadata Committee began work on revising Best Practices documentation in 2012 in collaboration with representatives from BookNet Canada. The 2013 publication of *Best Practices for Product Metadata* represents many months of work by the Committee. The publication offers accepted guidelines for the use of standards and for communicating book information in ways that have proven to work best for the book industry and consumers.

It's an understatement to say that the publishing industry has experienced many changes since 2005. *Best Practices for Product Metadata* addresses the changes by providing additional guidance related to metadata for digital products. The new version also consolidates recommendations for senders and receivers into one document and includes sections on both ONIX 2.1 and ONIX 3.0.

Intended Audience

Best Practices for Product Metadata provides guidelines for businesses, organizations, and institutions that regularly send and /or receive book metadata in electronic formats. This includes publishers, wholesalers, retailers (both online and bricks-and-mortar), libraries and other organizations that have an ongoing publishing component.

Many of the recommendations (especially those relating to basic required metadata elements and the style and usage guidelines) can be helpful for self-published authors or small publishers with only a few titles. But keep in mind that the guidelines are largely geared toward those that manage ongoing data feeds as either senders or receivers of book metadata.

Best Practices for Product Metadata is free and available for download from the BISG website.

Structure and Format of Best Practices for Product Metadata

Document Structure

*Best Practices for Product Metadata i*s strongly tied to ONIX for Books and the order of metadata elements in the document corresponds to the order of metadata in the ONIX for Books product record. The metadata elements in the document can be grouped into a few broad categories of metadata that largely correspond to metadata "Blocks" in the ONIX record. The recommendations and guidelines in *Best Practices for Product Metadata* complement but are not a substitute for official ONIX for Books documentation.

Metadata Elements

The following groups represent types of metadata as ordered in the ONIX record. *Best Practices for Product Metadata* doesn't cover every possible element but gives recommendations and guidelines for the most important and commonly required metadata elements within the "Blocks."

Product Numbers

A valid product number is required in every ONIX for Books product record and is also a requirement for most metadata recipients. More than one number can be provided, including proprietary numbers, but ISBN-13 is the international standard for book products. ISBN is a subset of the Global Trade Item Number (GTIN) system, universally used in trading systems across multiple product types.

Included in Best Practices for Product Metadata

- **Product Identifiers**
ISBN, GTIN, UPC, DOI, ISMI, Proprietary

- **Bar Code Indicator**
Bar code information is generally expected for North American products.

Product Description

This is the heart of the record and includes metadata that expresses information about the book's physical or digital form along with metadata that fully describes the content of the book: format, title, contributor, edition, series, subject, etc

Included in Best Practices for Product Metadata

- **Product Form/Format**
- **Weight and Dimension**
- **Country of Manufacture**
- **Digital Rights Management**
- **Number of Pieces**
- **Collections: Sets, Series, Bundles**
- **Contributor, Contributor Biography, Country Code**
- **Edition Information**
- **Title**
- **Language of Product Content**
- **Page count/Running time/Extent**

Marketing Collateral Detail

This metadata concerns information or resources that support marketing of the product.

Included in Best Practices for Product Metadata

- **Textual Description of Product**
- **Digital Image of Product**
- **Prizes**

Publishing Detail

Publishing Detail includes metadata elements providing information about the publisher or publishers, publishing status, and rights.

Included in Best Practices for Product Metadata

- **Publisher/Imprint/Brand Name**
- **Publisher Status Code**
- **Publication Date**
- **Strict on Sale (SOS) Date**
- **Territorial Rights**

Related Material

Metadata elements here provide links to related works and related products.

Included in Best Practices for Product Metadata

- **Related Products**
Used to indicate a new edition that supersedes an older one, multiple versions of a product with the same content, or a product that is pat of a multipart product.

Product Supply

Product Supply metadata specifies a market, the publishing status of a product in that market, and the supply details of a product in that market.

Included in Best Practices for Product Metadata

- **Distributor/Vendor of Record**
- **Product Availability Code**
- **Return Code**
- **Publisher's Proprietary Discount**
- **Price**
- **Case pack/Carton quantity**

Document Format and Sections

The following sections of information are provided for each major metadata element covered in *Best Practices for Product Metadata*.

1. Definition and background.
2. Business case for supplying this metadata element.
3. Is this metadata element mandatory in all product records?
4. Schedule and timing: When, in the life cycle of a product, should this data element be supplied.
5. Notes for data recipients on this metadata element.
6. Notes on the applicability and use of this data element digital products.
7. Style and usage guide.
8. ONIX 2.1 guidelines for this data element.
9. ONIX 3.0 guidelines for this data element.

Differences in the Revised Version

1. The original BISG best practices documents, *Best Practices for Senders* and *Best Practices for Receivers*, have been combined into one document.
2. Each data element includes notes on applicability for use for digital products.
3. Each element includes guidelines for ONIX 2.1 and guidelines for ONIX 3.0, addressing any changes from version 2.1.

A Closer Look at Best Practices for One Metadata Element

Definition and Background

Title: *The complete name of a published product as it appears on the title page.*

The title page is the definitive source for both the main title and the subtitle of a book. Variant titles found on book covers, dust jackets, spines, half-title pages, etc. should not be supplied in product data records, except as alternative titles. Titles should be presented in the appropriate title case for the language of the title.

Subtitle: *A secondary or explanatory title that follows the main title.*

Subtitles are often intended to amplify the meaning of the main title and/or augment the meaning of the main title; important for search engine optimization; and very useful for distinguishing between identical or similar titles.

Title prefix: *A leading word or words that are normally omitted when titles are alphabetized or index.*

Notes on Definition and Background

It might be assumed that "title" needs no definition. However, there's a lot of important information here. For example, the definition explains how to establish the definitive title when several might be printed on the book. Multiple senders often distribute records for the same title. Playing by the same metadata rules ensures the title will be displayed consistently on all user platforms, making it more likely to be found. Alternative titles can also be sent but rules make it more likely that the primary title will be the same regardless who's sending the metadata.

Business Case

The title of a product is often the most prominent piece of data about that product. The importance of an accurate, complete title cannot be overestimated. Incorrect or incomplete title data results in incorrect orders being placed by booksellers and incorrect books being purchased by consumers. Transmitting an accurate title for every item it wishes to sell is a key step in a publisher's efforts to ensure that its trading partners and end consumers will order the correct products.

Notes on Business Case

Most publishing industry participants don't need to be convinced that the title is important, but there are some metadata elements for which an understanding of the reasons that piece of metadata is important to the market can be helpful. And, although the importance of including a title is recognized by most, it's surprising how often title metadata is incorrect or inconsistent across versions of a title and senders of a title.

Is this mandatory data?

Yes, Every product, regardless of it's product form, should have a title. Even non-book products such as bookends should have a title (e.g., Antique Italian Wood Globe Bookends). At a minimum, a main title is mandatory for every product; subtitles and title prefixes should be supplied as applicable.

Notes on Mandatory Data

What is meant by mandatory? Best practice recommendations for mandatory elements are based on several criteria, including the following:

1. The majority of senders will not accept a record that is missing this piece of metadata.
2. It's a mandatory piece of data in a commonly used metadata communication format, such as ONIX for Books.
3. It has been deemed mandatory in metadata certification programs such as those administered by BISG, BookNet Canada, and BIC.

Following best practices for mandatory elements ensures that product metadata files will be accepted by the majority of industry trading partners.

When should this data be supplied?

A title, even if it is only a preliminary title, should be supplied 180 days prior to the on-sale date of a product. Preliminary or working titles should be updated to final titles no later than 120 days prior to the on-sale date.

Notes on Timing of Data Supply

Although it's not always possible for quick-to-market titles, mainstream publishers usually have title lists planned this far in advance. The number of pre-publication title changes is surprising and getting those changes to the market sometimes gets lost in the production process.

Style and Usage Guide (Excerpts)

Title

All books have a main title, but not all books have a subtitle. The title field should never carry extraneous information such as edition detail or Product Form; the latter should be carried in their own specialized data filed.

The appropriate title case for titles published in the English language is headline style. Per the Chicago Manual of Style, the following rules should be applied:
• The first and last words and all other major words (nouns, pronouns, adjectives, verbs, adverbs) and subordinating conjunctions are capitalized.
• Articles (a, an, the), coordinating conjunctions (and, but, or, for, nor), and prepositions, regardless of length, are lowercased unless they are the first or last word of the title or subtitle.
• Lowercase the part of a proper name that would be lowercased in text—e.g., de or von.

In titles that contain subtitles, the first portion of the title (i.e., the part of the title that appears before the subtitle) is referred to as the main title.

Notes on Title Style and Usage Guide

Style and usage sections can be lengthy. Don't take it for granted that the style and usage guidelines for each element are known and commonly applied! The style and usage guide for each element applies to metadata distributed in any format. Incorrect style can have a detrimental effect on how metadata is displayed to consumers in the marketplace and therefore on discovery and sales.

Some style guidelines simply reference and remind the user of English-language rules for expressing a title or other metadata elements. It's helpful in and of itself to have this document for specific reference without going to *Chicago Manual of Style* or other general reference works. But not all titles are in English and the rules differ for various languages. It's important to authors, publishers, and consumers of non-English language titles that the rules for that language are understood and reflected in product records.

The style and usage guide section for Title is not displayed here in its entirety. Following instead are general guidelines and a few examples. Errors in this essential field are more common than might be expected and can have a major impact on the effectiveness of online search and discovery. The following excerpts may shed some light on how errors can occur.

Title Examples

The Age of Innocence
Article as the first word of a title is capitalized

Of Time and the River
Preposition as the first word of a title is capitalized

And This Too Shall Pass
Coordinating conjunction as the first word of a title is capitalized

All about Us
About, when used as a preposition, is not capitalized

About Schmidt
About, when used as a preposition that is the first word of a title, is capitalized

Gone With the Wind
With is often capitalized in the title of this novel

Foreign Language Titles

In titles published in Spanish and French, the first word of the title and of the subtitle and all proper nouns should be capitalized. All other words should be lowercased.

Notes on Foreign Language Titles

Not all titles are in English and the rules differ for various languages. It's important to authors, publishers, and consumers of non-English language titles that the rules for that language are understood and reflected in product records.

Foreign Language Title Examples

El amor en los tiempos del cólera
Article as the first word of the title is capitalized in Spanish

El ingenioso hidalgo don Quijote de la Mancha
Proper names are capitalized in Spanish titles; titles of persons [e.g., don, señora, señor, etc.] are not capitalized

Title Prefix

In most Western European languages, titles with leading articles are alphabetized not by the leading article but by the first "important" word in the title.

Notes on Title Prefix

Title prefixes are handled differently in different languages as well. Errors in correctly identifying the title prefix can cause problems in indexing that affect search and discovery. Exceptions in rules for the title prefix can be problematic and also affect search and discovery.

Title Prefix Examples

A, An, The *(in English titles)*

El, La, Las, Lo, Los, Un, Una, Unas, Unos
(in Spanish titles)

La, Le, Les, L', Un, Une *(in French titles)*

Title Exceptions

There are exceptions to this rule of parsing out leading articles and placing them in the title prefix field. Titles that begin with place names are alphabetized under the place name, and therefore the leading articles in these titles should sometimes be placed in the main title data element.

The rule that applies in English-speaking regions is that place names beginning with an article usually do not drop that leading article for alphabetization purposes when the place name is not of English origin. For example, many place names in the United States are of French or Spanish origin, and such names that begin with articles are alphabetized under the article.

A second class of titles that may appear to violate the title prefix rule described above are books whose titles begin with the letter "A" used as a stand-alone letter, not as an indefinite article. In such titles the letter "A" should be placed in the Main Title data element and not in the Title Prefix data element

Title Exception Examples

A Is for Alibi

A: A Novel

A to Z of American Women Writers

Los Angeles: Biography of a City
"Los" should go into the Main Title data element

Las Vegas: A Photographic Tour
"Las" should go into the Main Title data element

El Paso: Local Frontiers at a Global Crossroads
"El" should go into the Main Title data element

La Grange and La Grange Park Illinois
"La" should go into the Main Title data element

ONIX 2.1 Guidelines (Excerpts)

Suppliers of product data should use the Title Composite data element.

Reference name: `<Title>`
Short tag: `<title>`
Any occurrence of the `<Title>` composite must include one of the following (**a** or **b**):

a. PR.7.11 Title Text
Format: Variable-length text, suggested maximum 300 characters
Reference name: `<TitleText>`
Short tag: `<b203>`
This data element should be used for products that do not have a title prefix (i.e., a leading article).

b. PR.7.12 Title Prefix
Format: Variable-length text, suggested maximum length 20 characters
Reference name: `<TitlePrefix>`
Short tag: `<b030>`

The `<Title>` composite must also include:

PR.7.13 Title Text Without Prefix
Format: Variable-length text, suggested maximum length 300 characters
Reference name: `<TitleWithoutPrefix>`
Short tag: `<b031>`
The combination of these two data elements should be used for products that have a title prefix.

In addition, the following data element is mandatory within the Title Composite.

PR.7.8 Title Type Code
Format: Fixed-length, 2 numeric digits
Reference name: `<TitleType>`
Short tag: `<b202>`

Code list: List 15
The value from Code List 15 should be one of the following:

01 Distinctive Title
The full text of the distinctive title of the item, without further abbreviation or abridgement.
03 Title in original language
Original title for a work in translation.
08 Former Title
A title different from the Distinctive Title that was used in a previous publication of the work.
10 Distributor's Title
The title carried in a book distributor's title file; it is frequently truncated or incomplete, and may include elements that are not properly part of the title.

Titles that contain a subtitle, including alternatives to distinctive titles such as Former Title, require the use of an additional data element within the Title Composite:

PR.7.14 Subtitle
Format: Variable-length text, suggested maximum 300 characters
Reference name: `<Subtitle>`
Short tag: `<b029>`

Notes on ONIX Guidelines

Best Practices for Product Metadata ONIX Guidelines are not a replacement for official ONIX documentation and guidelines published by EDItEUR and available from their website. These sections provide reference and recommendations for commonly used components of the ONIX record. Guidelines are consistent with ONIX guidelines and informed by input from the U.S. and Canadian publishing communities.

ONIX 3.0 Guidelines (Excerpts)

ONIX 3.0 has a very different approach to the use of the Title field, because 3.0 takes into account the possibility of providing collection titles as well as product-level titles. However, detailed advice given here regarding capitalization, prefixes, title types, subtitles and the textcase attribute all apply equally to ONIX 3.0. Extensive information and instructions for using this data element in ONIX 3.0 are available on the EDItEUR website:

Title Detail Composite

A repeatable group of data elements which together give the text of a title and specify its type.

P.6.1 Title type code
An ONIX code indicating the type of a title. P.6.1a Title element sequence number (new in 3.0.1)
A number which specifies a single overall sequence

of title elements, which is the preferred order for display of the various title elements when constructing a complete title.

Title Element Composite

A repeatable group of data elements which together represent an element of a title.

P.6.2 Title element level
An ONIX code indicating the level of a title element: collection level, subcollection level, or product level. Mandatory in each occurrence of the `<TitleElement>` composite, and non-repeating.

P.6.3 Part number
P.6.4 Year of annual
P.6.5 Title text
P.6.6 Title prefix
P.6.7 Title without prefix
P.6.8 Subtitle
P.6.8a Title statement (new in 3.0.1)
Free text showing how the overall title ... should be presented in any display ...

Notes on ONIX 3.0 Guidelines

New in the revised version, ONIX 3.0 Guidelines provide a quick reference to any differences between version 2.1 and version 3.0.

Although many metadata senders and recipients continue to use ONIX 2.1, most are transitioning to ONIX 3.0 since full support for version 2.1 will end January 2014.

As the excerpts demonstrate, there are some significant differences in version 3.0 for Title metadata. For some metadata elements, there are no significant differences or changes.

The excerpt here points out a specific difference In ONIX 3.0 relating to title types. A product record may contain multiple titles, the title of the series (collection-level) and the title of the book (product-level), for example. The metadata must indicate the title type.

ONIX 3.0 allows expression of multiple title types and also allows the user to define the order in which the title elements will be displayed. Not all of the elements will be needed for every title.

Users should refer to ONIX 3.0 documentation available on the EDitEUR website for extensive guidance on creating title metadata.

. . . .

The best way to learn best practices is by using them. The DataCurate Metadata Quick Guide titled *Metadata Best Practices and Industry Certification* expands on this chapter and provides exercises allowing hands-on use of BISG's *Product Metadata Best Practices.* This publication is available for purchase from Digital Book World.

Download the Metadata Best Practices & Indsutry Certification PDF

Integrating *Best Practices* into Organizational Workflows

Metadata underlies many parts of the publishing process. *Best Practices for Product Metadata* can be used or adapted as a reference for staff creating, entering, or editing book metadata in any division, as well as for staff responsible for metadata distribution in ONIX or other electronic file formats.

Anyone dealing with product description or metadata distribution should be familiar with the document's structure and format so that questions arising in everyday activities can be answered quickly. Depending on job responsibilities, some staff members may refer often to style guidelines but rarely to ONIX guidelines and vice versa.

Staff responsible for data mining, data interpretation, and business intelligence should understand the organization's metadata components and metadata flow. Metadata that works supports all aspects of publishing.

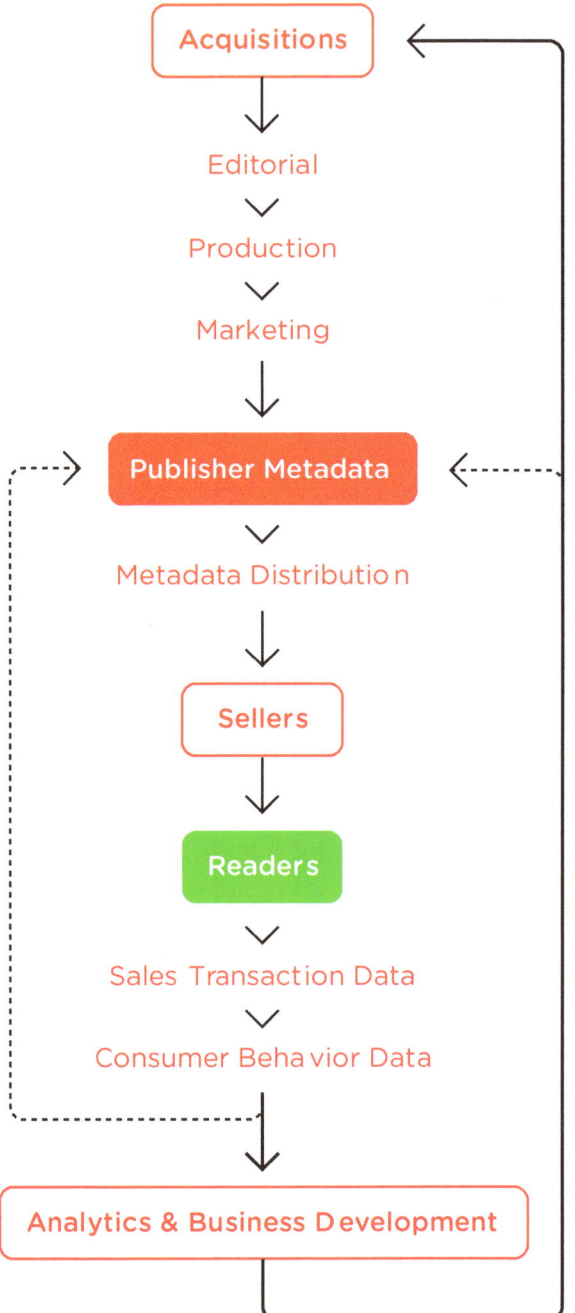

Chapter 14: Metadata Certification Programs

What is Certification?

Accurate and timely metadata sells books and creates efficiencies across the publisher supply chain. Book industry organizations In the U.S., Canada, and the UK developed certification programs to give publishers and other metadata providers the opportunity for feedback on metadata completeness and quality with the goal of increasing metadata quality across the industry.

Certification of a publisher's metadata also gives their supply chain partners a degree of comfort that ongoing metadata feeds will meet their system and business needs without extensive review of each file.

Certification programs evaluate metadata files against standard industry benchmarks and file validation criteria resulting in recognized metadata certification for metadata senders with acceptable scores.

The BISG Product Certification Program (PDCP)

PDCP is a voluntary program in which independent experts evaluate and rank metadata for compliance to industry standards and best practices. The program is free and open to all suppliers of product metadata. Metadata submitted to PDCP is evaluated against the criteria found in *Best Practices for Product Metadata*, including the presence or absence of the mandatory metadata elements defined in the document.

Metadata files, submitted in either ONIX or Excel, are evaluated by a certification panel supervised by BISG. The panel includes representatives from major North American metadata recipients, including Barnes & Noble, Bowker, Ingram, and the Library of Congress.

The Evaluation Process

Files undergo a three-part evaluation process.

1. Checks for valid file structure.
ONIX files are checked for conformance with EDitEUR's DTD and valid XML structure. Excel files are checked for conformance with an industry-provided template for metadata in Excel.

2. Checks for the presence or absence of mandatory data elements.
Eighty percent of the supplier's records must meet criteria before being passed on for further evaluation and scoring. Some mandatory elements that are expected to be present in post-publication metadata are not expected in metadata for forthcoming titles. Quantitative scores take this into consideration based on the publication date. For example, page count for books or running time for audio may not be available pre-publication.

3. Certification Panel Review
If a file meets the minimum score of 80%, the certification panel will review a representative sample of records for quality. Sixteen fields are reviewed for accuracy and adherence to best practices. All scores are confidential.

Fields Reviewed by the PDCP Certification Panel

The following metadata elements are evaluated for correct usage and format recommended by *Best Practices for Product Metadata*. Not all elements are applicable to all products and omission of elements not applicable to the product will not affect the score.

- Title
- Contributor(s)
- Publisher/Imprint/Brand Name
- Price
- Publisher Status Code
- Publication Date
- Product Availability Code
- Product Form/Format/Binding
- Strict On Sale (SOS) Date
- BISAC Subject Code(s)
- Language(s) of Product Content
- Collection/Series
- Volume Number/Set
- Edition
- ONIX Audience Code
- Age Range
- Textual Description of Product
- Illustration Details
- Digital Image of Product

Product Data Certification in Other Countries

BISG's PDCP program and *Best Practices for Product Metadata* were developed in coordination with BookNet Canada. Data files certified by PDCP will be acceptable to BookNet Canada. Programs in the UK (BIC Basic) and Australia (APA) require some data points (BIC Subject Codes, for example) specific to those markets, but measurements for common data points are compatible.

Levels of Certification

Product metadata is certified at three levels: Gold, Silver, and Bronze, with additional levels for excellence within each of the three categories. Participating in PDCP and receiving certification sends a message to the industry that an organization is committed to the implementation of industry standards and best practices and contributes to the quality of metadata in the marketplace.

Find out more **about the BISG Product Data Certification Program.**

National Publishing Industry Organizations

UNITED STATES	**CANADA**	**UNITED KINGDOM**
Book Industry Study Group (BISG)	BookNet Canada (BNC)	Book Industry Communication (BIC)
www.bisg.org	*www.booknetcanada.ca*	*www.bic.org.uk*

Description

BISG is a national, not-for-profit book trade association committed to the development of industry standards, best practices, research and events for the publishing industry.	BNC provides support to the publisher supply chain through products and services in support of standards and technology for bibliographic data, electronic data exchange, and business data.	BIC is an independent organization promoting e supply chain efficiency in all sectors of the book world through e-commerce and the application of standard processes and procedures.

Membership, Leadership & Funding

BISG is mainly funded by membership dues. BISG membership represents all segments of the book industry. Individuals and independent consultants may also join. BISG's Board of Directors is comprised of a cross-section of senior executives from across the book industry.	BNC has the financial support of the Government of Canada through the Canadian Book Fund (CBF). BNC's Board of Directors includes broad representation through the industry.	BIC is mainly funded by membership dues. Membership is open to all organizations involved in the book trade and library supply chains. Individuals and independent consultants may also join. The Board and Operational Board members include representatives from the publisher supply chain and libraries.

Membership Fee

Annual dues for various levels are determined by size (revenue) and type of business. **Price range:** From $595 for individuals and libraries to $25,000 for Gold Sponsors.	Financial support is through the Canadian Book Fund (CBF).	Annual dues for various levels are determined by size (revenue) and type of business. **Price range:** From £70 for an individual or library to £6,095 for a patron membership.

national publishing industry organizations (con't)

UNITED STATES	CANADA	UNITED KINGDOM
Book Industry Study Group (BISG)	BookNet Canada (BNC)	Book Industry Communication (BIC)

Products: Subject & Classification

· BISAC Subject Headings · BISAC Merchandising Themes · BISAC Regional Themes	BISAC Subject Headings, available from **BISG,** are the North American standard and are used by the Canadian book industry.	· BIC Standard Subject Categories · Children's Book Marketing Classifications · E4Libraries Subject Category Headings

Products: Publications, Tools & Services

· ***Book Industry Trends*** · ***BookStats*** · Standards and best practices documentation. · Frequent reports and research publications.	· ***Canadian Book Market*** (Annual publication) · Various reports and research publications. · **CataList** – Online catalog system · **BiblioShare** – Data aggregation service for ONIX, image, and position files. · **SalesData** – Tracks data from over 1,000 sources to help predict trends and manage inventory.	· Standards and best practices documentation. · Frequent reports and research publications.

Annual Events

· Making Information Pay · Making Information Pay for Higher Education · Annual Members Meeting	· BNC Technology Forum	· London Book Fair Supply Chain Seminar · New Trends

Seminars, Webinars & Training

BISG offers frequent webcasts on industry topics.	BNC offers occasional training programs, webinars, and seminars. They also maintain a blog and an e-newsletter.	BIC provides frequent training opportunities in collaboration with the Publishing Training Center.

Accreditation & Certification Programs

Product Data Certification Program	Bibliographic Certification Program	· BIC Product Data Excellence Awards · BIC Supply Chain Excellence Awards · BIC e4libraries Accreditation

Part 5: Metadata and the Future of Publishing

Chapter 15: Trends in Book Publishing and Metadata

In the first edition of the *Handbook*, we asked four questions of industry leaders.

1. What is the most important metadata challenge facing publishers/libraries today?
2. What actions are publishers/libraries are taking to address the challenge?
3. If you could choose a first-priority action needed, what would it be?
4. What outcomes would you like to see over the next 3-5 years?

For this edition, we asked our contributors if responses published in the first edition are still valid, or if they would like to update or revise any of their answers. In the individual responses that follow, we have indicated when responses are revised or new to this edition. The authors deeply appreciate these thoughtful contributions. The common themes identified in the first edition remain relevant and some have been added.

Common Themes from the First Edition

- Ongoing metadata creation and maintenance should be integrated into the overall publishing process. This will require new responsibilities and training but will result in increased publisher "ownership" and control of their metadata — a key organizational asset.

- The production and maintenance of ebook metadata should be fully integrated and consistent with print processes.

- Current systems often fail to meet 21st century metadata needs. These needs include:

  o Capacity and flexibility to handle the rapidly increasing volume of and dynamic nature of metadata.

  o Metadata management of multiple versions of a work rather than managing one product at a time.

  o Integration of print and digital metadata workflows.

  o The ability to support the full range of potential metadata elements and uses.

  o Functionality that allows robust and frequent communication with trading partners, including efficient, automated metadata export and ingest.

- Widespread adoption of industry standards and best practices facilitates the efficient flow of information, raises potential for automation, reduces redundancy and inconsistency, and increases metadata quality.

- There's a need for more communication and collaboration across the publisher supply chain and between the publishing industry and libraries.

- A movement toward "whole-industry" solutions is needed.

- The trend toward open data will continue. The publishing industry and the library community should move toward business models, metadata practices, and systems that support the potential of shared metadata, linked data, and increased metadata exposure.

- Exploiting the potential of identifiers to link bibliographic metadata, including names, can create business challenges but ultimately benefits all through increased discovery, a better user experience, and efficiencies in metadata management across the supply chain.

New to This Edition

- Migration from ONIX 2.1 to 3.0 is moving more slowly than anticipated, especially in the United States. Transition to the current version requires development and resources, but becomes more urgent as support for 2.1 ends and a significant percentage of the international community uses 3.0.

- There are even more opportunities (and reasons) to leverage metadata and build metadata structures in support of better search and discovery for publishers of all sizes and types. The full potential of ONIX 3.0 should be utilized to capture and communicate more metadata elements.

- The potential advantages of embedding more metadata in actual content (digital files) should be aggressively explored and more fully utilized.

- Schema.org will become increasingly important through its ability to associate metadata with granular components of content, from a chapter to a word or phrase.

- Effective rights management through the use of metadata is becoming more and more important.

Len Vlahos
Executive Director, Book Industry Study Group

Second Edition Update

Len Vlahos provided the following update to his responses from the first edition. Information about accessing the documents Len mentions can be found in the Bibliography and References section.

It's been a busy time for BISG and metadata since we last answered questions for the Metadata Handbook. Among other things:

- Our Metadata Committee (chaired by Richard Stark of Barnes & Nobel) worked with our colleagues at BookNet Canada to revise our Product Metadata Best Practices (and we are already updating it again!);
- We published Best Practices for Keywords in Metadata, a widely read and well-received guide to using metadata to improve discoverability;
- We published Recommendations for Citing Common Core State Standards in ONIX;
- We launched a working group (chaired by Chris Saynor of Giant Chair/ONIXSuite) to address the migration from ONX 2.1 to ONIX 3.0;
- We launched a working group (chaired by Graham Bell of EDItEUR) to create a mapping between key elements of ONIX and Schema.org, the standard for communicating metadata on the open Web;
- We launched an educational taxonomies working group (co-chaired by Connie Harbison of Baker & Taylor and Pat Payton of Bowker) to continue the work begun by the Common Core working group noted above;
- We're also in the final phase of retooling our product data certification program. We're again partnering with BookNet Canada to bring low cost, very reliable ONIX validation tools to our members. We expect to launch in beta in Q1 or Q2 of this year;

Metadata and discoverability continue to be ground zero for much of the work BISG is doing. We encourage those with an interest in book product metadata to join BISG and to participate in our committees and working groups.

.....

What is the most important metadata challenge facing publishers and/or libraries today?

While BISG is not a publisher (or library!) the metadata report we recently released — Development, Use, and Modification of Book Product Metadata (prepared for us by Magellan Media Partners) — highlighted a number of challenges publishers are facing with regard to metadata. First and foremost is communication. We, as an industry, need to communicate better with one another about product data. From acceptance of and adherence to common terminology, to better information about changes to existing records, we can greatly help the quality of metadata if we get better at talking to one another.

What actions are publishers and/or libraries are taking to address the challenge?

Through industry groups like BISG, publishers and libraries can participate in an ongoing dialogue about a variety of standards and best practices, including those surrounding metadata. At BISG, we have a standing committee that deals with metadata, including the preparation and updating of best practice documents for both metadata senders and recipients.

If you could choose a first-priority action needed, what would it be?

I think the industry needs to convene a metadata congress of sorts, with willing participants from all corners of the supply chain. There are problems that can be solved by implementing consistent business processes between trading partners, and again (not to sound like a broken record), through better communication. Groups like BISG, BNC, BIC, and EDItEUR can play a role in making this happen.

What outcomes would you like to see over the next 3-5 years?

In addition to better communication, my hope is that we see a large scale move to ONIX 3.0 in the U.S. One of the key features of 3.0 is the ability to send updates for only those records or portion of records that change. This alone will cut down wasted effort and data bloat. Besides, EDItEUR will stop supporting ONIX 2.1 in 2014, so the time to begin the migration is now!

....

Noah Genner
CEO and President, BookNet Canada

Second Edition Update

Noah Genner's original responses remain relevant today.

....

What is the most important metadata challenge facing publishers/libraries today?

I think the biggest change that they both face is likely process change. How do they change the way they do things now to make it easier for them, to gain advantage, or to just stay relevant in changing times? Analyzing what they do and being able to see opportunities to do it better is the challenge — for metadata and beyond. For metadata I think there are some more specific challenges for each:

- **Publishers**: Dealing with so many different channels (i.e. libraries, print retailers, digital retailers, discoverability platforms, etc.) who don't always have the same wants/needs, or much in the way of 'book knowledge'.
- **Libraries**: Getting and using the most current data. (We are much more focused on the publisher and retailer sides of the metadata world.)

What actions are publishers/libraries taking to address the challenge?

Publishers are thinking of metadata as much more than just a supply-chain tool and starting to get other departments/people involved in creating and maintaining the data. Also, they are starting to embed the processes for creating, and updating, metadata into their publishing workflows.

If you could choose a first-priority action needed, what would it be?

Keep it dynamic and build the metadata workflow into your 'regular' workflow. Metadata drives consumer/reader awareness and keeping it current is incredibly important.

What outcomes would you like to see over the next 3-5 years?

That dynamic and rich (content and context) metadata is easily made available to all players in the book supply chain. That the metadata can be used to power cool book/content projects to drive reader discovery.

Pat Payton
Senior Manager, Public Relations and Content Development, Bowker

Second Edition Update

Pat Payton's responses to the original questions remain relevant. She also identified aggregator handling of three metadata initiatives – ONIX 3.0, ISNI, and Thema – as an important issue, so a new question with Pat's comments regarding these initiatives is added at the end of this section.

....

What is the most important metadata challenge facing publishers today?

As recently as five years ago, metadata was often handled by the editorial or IT staff. Now metadata is often handled by the sales and marketing staff. Yet, there is pressure to sell books versus create and update metadata. In reality as we move more toward digital products these are not separate tasks. In the interim, publishers are facing these limitations:

- Finding the manpower to apply effort to metadata
- Knowing where to start in order to do a better job at metadata for new books
- Tackling issues with older metadata
- Separate systems for ebook and print data

What actions are aggregators taking to address the challenge?

Bowker tries to support publishers of all sizes by being flexible in the way we accept data. We also try to assist publishers while they attempt to create Excel or ONIX feeds by answering questions and providing detail feedback on data samples. By participating in industry conferences, webinars, and projects such as this one we aim to open discussions with publishers in order to see what their pain points are and to aid them in their effort to improve their metadata.

If you could choose a first-priority action needed, what would it be?

Publishers should assign time to regularly focus on metadata and not think of it as an extra task to be delegated to lower level staff or put off because it seems like an onerous task. It is easy to get started when you approach it from a sales perspective. Because potential readers discover their next book through word of mouth, bookstores, libraries, the media, and many other places, publishers should concentrate on the data fields that offer the most discoverability for an item. Think of the customer's experience and work from there:

- What would cause them to become interested in a title? Title, Series Title, Cover Image, Contributor, Contributor Biography, Multiple BISAC subject codes or Keywords, Description of the work, Table of Contents
- Once they find a title, what do they need to know to acquire it? ISBN, Format, Price, Supplier, Status, Publication Date

By answering these questions with accurate and complete metadata, a publisher is headed in the right direction. Approach the task in phases such as ensuring next season's titles are all complete and correct or build up from a small set of data fields each season by adding a new field.

What outcomes would you like to see over the next 3-5 years?

I feel that publishers should aim for a more integrated approach between ebook and print metadata. Print data is often more complete. Ebook metadata is handled through different systems and often times there is not a complete list of all ebooks available in a single feed. (Bowker often finds that certain titles are only sold through particular channels and their metadata is only available in that retailer's template rather than a publisher's central database.) Cover images are forgotten and thought to be part of the ebook itself so no separate marketing image is needed. All of these issues can be address if a publisher integrates their workflow for these two formats. Integrated workflows exist for print and audio and since ebook growth is showing that the format is here to stay, publishers should make the leap in order to improve the metadata and save time.

Added Question for Second Edition

How are aggregators dealing with the metadata initiatives such as ONIX 3, Thema, and ISNI?

These are three major metadata initiatives that all industry players, including aggregators and publishers, are analyzing and acting on today. Each of them require a significant amount of resources and a change in database structures. Mostly it is a matter of allocating resources to determine the development work needed to support each new scheme/identifier and then prioritizing which initiative will be picked up in the marketplace first. The momentum of the marketplace is the key factor in identifying the order of these projects.

Take ONIX 3 as an example. We can start by reviewing the historical development of ONIX 2.0 and 2.1. Since 2007, when on average 50% of the metadata suppliers were sending spreadsheet or text format, In 2014, ONIX is almost 80% of what metadata suppliers are using. The increase has been steady over time. Both the 20% of the market that has never created ONIX and the 80% already comfortable with ONIX could move over to ONIX 3. However, the full migration will most likely take years to complete.

Next, we look to the marketplace to get feedback from publishers and other aggregators. Bowker generally follows the Book Industry Study Group's *Product Metadata Best Practices*. We actively participate in the relevant committees and working groups that draft these practices and are invested in making adjustments to our system to accept new data points. Over time, these best practices have assisted publishers in adopting similar practices in sending their data and have provided a roadmap they can use to improve and expand metadata including guidance on moving to ONIX 3. BISG has also been offering training sessions for publishers to learn more about the transition from ONIX 2.1 to 3. This tells us that many publishers are gaining knowledge on how ONIX 3 works.

Finally, Bowker conducted a survey earlier this year on our metadata providers' plans for ONIX 3. Through that survey, we found that the largest issue (63% of respondents) with ONIX 3 implementation and planning was that no customers are requesting ONIX 3. The second most popular issue (39%) was conflicting business priorities that keep postponing the development of ONIX 3. Keeping these results in mind, we can see that the movement will most likely be slow, but the momentum is there. Bowker is in the process of programming our ONIX 3 ingest and has already created a mapped version of ONIX 3 for our customer base.

Wendell Lotz
Vice President, Metadata, Ingram Book Group

Second Edition Update

Wendell Lotz provided the following updated answers to the original questions.

What is the most important metadata challenge facing publishers/libraries today?

Three years ago I answered this question in the light of a growing ebook industry which was frequently building metadata records through separate process chains from those used by the print owner of the content. Audio book metadata was particularly poor in relation to the print book from which the audio was derived. The records produced by the ebook and print arms of major publishers were frequently different even when the publisher was the same. Now, I believe most publishers have seen the need to, at the least, deliver the same metadata descriptions for the various formats in their domain.

The challenge now, for the industry as a whole, is building structures to allow search, discovery, and browsability, not only for the small press and the self-published author but also for houses of all sizes. We have a chance, through our metadata tools, to make titles from the smaller publishers, nearly as findable as those titles from the major publishers. It will take even more robust records as well as the talents of librarians and retailers to use them.

What actions are publisher/libraries taking to address the challenge?

Publishers who truly value metadata, and understand what quality metadata can mean to the increase of their sales, are broadening the number of attributes they are covering. For them there are regular and ongoing projects that evolve their coverage of the different elements available to them in the ONIX standard. I have always believed the Best Practices are 'aspirational.' There are no metadata 'police'; indeed, no publisher is likely to launch their ONIX offerings with all the data fields that are desired. Currently our receipts of ONIX files indicate efforts to cover Country of Publication, Place of Publication, keywords, brand names, age ranges, and reading levels to their attribute coverage.

More and more publishers are using one of the several metadata services companies offering software and other tools to assist the publisher in building quality records and distributing them to trading partners. At my company, with an assignment to capture new and current elements on ONIX records, we received 65% of the over 50 million ONIX records we processed last year from just five DAM/DAD service providers.

If you could choose a first-priority action needed, what would it be?

With the sunset of ONIX 2.1 nearly upon us (12/31/2014) it behooves all trading partners to move expeditiously to Version 3.0. The new version provides numerous advantages to the current version and further offers many new features such as Collections coverage and more flexible and expanded ebook coverage. Use of Version 3.0 will facilitate the merger of the print and ebook processes recommended in the first question above.

What outcomes would you like to see over the next 3-5 years?

I would like to see at least an 80% adoption of ONIX 3.0 at the title level with a similar number of publishers certified by the BISG certification process. In addition I would urge publishers and recipients to develop to the maintenance of revised records according to the Version 3.0 standard, which permits the sending of one or more blocks of data rather than the entire record when only a few elements are changing. Currently nearly 90% of the records we process contain only minor changes. As the title count grows and selling is done online where there is no shelf space limit, communication of the changes in metadata will need to occur in smaller files, or web services.

Bill Kasdorf

Vice President, Apex Content Solutions, Metadata Subgroup Lead, IDPF EPUB 3 Working Group

Second Edition Update

While his original responses remain valid, Bill Kasdorf provides additional comments at the end of this section.

The biggest challenge — and opportunity — is what I call Mainstreaming Metadata. Too often, metadata is seen as a specialized, technical aspect of publishing that is "somebody else's job." In reality, everybody in the publishing value chain — from authoring to acquisition, development, editing, production, manufacturing, marketing, sales, and distribution — not only works with metadata every day (whether they realize it or not), but depends on metadata, or suffers from the lack of it. Metadata is the lubricant that makes the whole process work smoothly.

Not only does everybody have an interest in it, each participant in the value chain needs to recognize which kinds of metadata they need to take responsibility for. This can include descriptive metadata (from simple keywords to BISAC codes or LC subject headings), administrative metadata ("Do we have electronic rights to this image?" "In what countries can this book be sold?"), technical metadata ("This is the high-res grayscale .tiff, I need the color .jpeg and a thumbnail"), structural metadata ("You can view the abstract for free," "I want to use this chapter in my course") etc.

Everybody in the publishing ecosystem has an interest in — and should take responsibility for — some of these aspects of metadata being correct and cur- rent. Marketing folks need to know that, in production, the author decided to use her middle initial. Customers need to know that this EPUB has been optimized for iBooks, that one has been optimized for the Nook. Sure, developing systems to manage metadata better are important, and using standards (let's get on with ONIX 3.0, already!) is critical, but at the end of the day the key is recognizing that good metadata is everybody's job and in everybody's interest.

Added Comments for Second Edition

While my comments above from the previous edition of this book are every bit as valid now as they were then, I'm glad to have the opportunity to point out a few more things that I think have become increasingly relevant with regards to metadata.

The Discovery Imperative: For publishers who are in the business of selling content, metadata for _discovery_ is really their top priority. While those publishers do now commonly provide extensive metadata in their ONIX feeds to the supply chain, it is increasingly evident that this is necessary but not sufficient. Those ONIX feeds are separate from the content itself, and for most book publishers, the content itself is not actually online at all. But in many sectors of publishing, the content itself is increasingly online: scholarly journals and books, textbooks (perhaps in a platform like VitalSource, not on the open Web), magazines, and even aggregations and portals of content from trade books. In this context, schema.org will become increasingly important. It enables associating metadata with arbitrarily granular components of content, from a chapter to a word or phrase. The ever-expanding set of properties and vocabularies available in schema.org now includes metadata for education and accessibility; and BISG is launching an initiative to assess what aspects of ONIX can (or should be able to) be expressed via schema.org.

The Chunking Imperative: For some types of publishers, the opportunity to derive additional income not from whole publications but from parts of them is becoming not only attractive but practical. In order to do this, they need good metadata—both structural ("this is a chapter," "this is a quiz," "this is a recipe") and content semantics ("this chunk is about Italian cuisine," "this chunk is about XYZ corporation")—associated not only at the title or publication level but at more granular levels within the content. Having good XML or XHTML—ideally based on HTML5, which is finally an official W3C Recommendation—provides an important foundation for this.

The International Imperative: The digital revolution has broken down the geographical barriers we have come to take for granted and has made it much easier to sell or distribute content anywhere in the world. Metadata plays a key role in facilitating this. Using international standards like ONIX provides a lingua franca: while the English terms in ONIX may be a barrier for some cultures, the corresponding numbers are not. And while most subject metadata schemes like BISAC and BIC are geographically specific, the new Thema scheme is truly international (and enables localization as well).

The Rights Imperative: All of the above also makes it ever more important to be able to associate rights metadata—both human-readable and, even more urgently, machine-readable metadata—with those granular chunks of content. What rights do I have for this image in this book I published in print and am now issuing as an e-book? How much of this e-book that I just acquired can I legally share, if any? Can I print this out. In my view, it is one of the most urgent priorities of the industry to develop open, robust, sufficiently expressive metadata standards for rights expression that can work across all publishing sectors—trade, education, magazines, news, and STM.

The Metadata Imperative: I can't resist closing with this no-brainer. Every year, the importance of metadata becomes clearer and clearer throughout the publishing ecosystem.

....

Graham Bell

Executive Director, EDItEUR

Second Edition Update

Graham Bell provided the following updated version of his original responses.

....

What is the most important metadata challenge facing publishers/libraries today?

Put simply, *change*. Most publishers use metadata management processes and IT systems that weren't designed for today's business world.

More than ever, each product a publisher wants to sell needs complete, accurate and timely metadata. Managing the growing number of products is a challenge that's taxing the capacity of many publisher IT systems. Managing metadata one product at a time is expensive, but that's how most publisher's systems work, because they were designed for a world in which there were just one or two versions of each title ('manifestations of each work'). The nature of the publishing business is changing, and there are now often many more than two versions of each title. So the challenge is to create systems that allow publishing staff to manage the metadata in a more efficient, relational fashion: correcting the author's name or assigning the subject category should change the name or category on all versions of that book, not just on a single product.

Change is also reflected in the growing demands for a broader range of metadata elements for each product. As the book and e-book trade becomes more global, there's a premium put on better data about rights, for example, an area where few publishers can provide comprehensive data. While publishers often provide front cover images, few can also provide sample chapters, accurate back-cover blurb or tables of contents. The shift to online bookselling means metadata is all you have, and it needs at least to replicate as far as possible the experience of physical browsing. But with richer, more structured and more granular metadata, online bookselling can in addition offer a unique, smarter retail experience.

Business models are changing too: publishers are experimenting with subscriptions, with rentals and with bundling of various types, and these experiments raise new challenges for metadata management, because of the many different routes to market for a single 'book'. Delivering metadata in bulk to data aggregators and retailers isn't the only thing publishers need to focus on, and the use of machine-readable structured metadata on the internet — within ordinary web pages, in search engines and so on — is of increasing importance.

And metadata itself is *dynamic*. A catalogue of products isn't a static document, as new products are added and older ones withdrawn. But neither is the data for a single product static: the metadata for a specific product changes — and needs to be managed — throughout that product's lifecycle.

Finally, the value of metadata has changed. Not long ago, publishing staff viewed metadata as a chore, an afterthought, not something that was critical to the sales of their books. Many still do. But when selling online, metadata is all you have, the core of the sales and marketing effort.

What actions are publishers are taking to address the challenge?

Those that understand the critical nature of metadata in enabling the supply chain and growing the sales of their products are integrating the creation of metadata more closely into their business processes, and are beginning to invest in new-generation metadata management applications that handle both print and e-book products in a more structured, comprehensive and efficient way. Some publishers are also recognizing the metadata is now the key element of their business-to-consumer communication, and shifting metadata ownership from editorial or production into sales and marketing.

If you could choose a first-priority action needed, what would it be?

Adopt a range of solutions that are already in place — ONIX 3.0, identifiers like ISTC and ISNI, and even linked data.

What outcomes would you like to see over the next 3–5 years?

- A growth in awareness among senior managers of the critical business value of metadata, and a changed view of metadata from 'chore to core'. This will lead publishers to invest in their systems, their staff and the processes that generate high-quality metadata.
- The broad adoption of key identifiers like ISTC and ISNI, in order to reduce the uncertainties of grouping products together. If clusters of products can be grouped reliably it means retailers can deliver a smarter online shopping experience and customers can make better, more informed decisions about which version of a title to buy.
- Full adoption of ONIX 3.0: it's the accepted global standard for book and e-book trade metadata, and is much better suited to the e-book trade than previous versions of ONIX.
- Greater understanding of the importance of metadata in online environments using linked data, RDFa or microdata syntaxes.
- A continued growth in the quality, richness and easy availability of the metadata delivered by publishers, and continued 'whole-industry' collaboration to ensure metadata communication is effective, efficient and relevant to evolving business needs.

Jonathan Nowell
President, Nielsen Book

Second Edition Update

Jonathan Nowell's original responses remain relevant today.

What is the most important metadata challenge facing publishers/libraries today?

The biggest challenge today must be to continue to improve the discoverability of books online, ebooks in particular. There are two sides to discoverability: bringing the right products to the attention of the reader — "these are the type of books you are looking for"; and qualification — "this is the one you should read". I believe there is still a holy grail to be found in the form of the online book-browsing experience that is the equivalent of talking to a knowledgeable and informed bookseller or librarian. Many have tried, but it is very hard to pull off: what you need to achieve doesn't just take artificial intelligence, it needs artificial wisdom, which is hard.

What actions are publishers/libraries are taking to address the challenge?

To meet these challenges, publishers are extending the range of the metadata record with powerful new features: URL links for related material, inside spreads, audio, video clips, browse inside, sample chapters, etc. A challenge that remains is ensuring the widest possible dissemination and exposure of material of this kind.

If you could choose a first-priority action needed, what would it be?

In terms of priorities, today it must still be: "don't forget the basics". If you're spending money on author interviews or promotional videos but you haven't got a high quality, rich, comprehensive and accurate product record — up to the standards of your very best records — for every single pbook and ebook in your catalogue then, you have your priorities wrong. For pbooks metadata is crucial, for ebooks it is critical.

Interesting to note, when we did a survey of our users several years ago, the overwhelming top priority for new data functionality was the ability to reliably, definitively and automatically link all related editions. With greater proliferation of editions and versions of parallel products, that requirement is now even greater, and, the good news is, we are closing in on solutions.

What outcomes would you like to see over the next 3-5 years?

The goal for the longer term must be to get Metadata in front of users in the interfaces, platforms and workflows that they are using day in and day out. Metadata needs to become all-pervasive in the same way that the Internet has. It needs to move from being a destination — somewhere you go to, to being part of the environment — somewhere you are.

Laura Dawson
Technical Product Manager, Proquest

Second Edition Update

Laura Dawson's original responses remain relevant today.

What is the most important metadata challenge facing publishers/libraries today?

I think these are almost diametrically opposed. Of course, everyone is in favor of discovery. But publishers do not want patrons/consumers discovering books that they themselves did not publish; libraries want patrons to find everything that's relevant. If relevant books happen to be published by one publisher over another, that's not an issue for a library; it is for a publisher. This is some of the difficulty we are seeing around ISTC. Publishers don't want their books linked to other books that might be more tempting.

What actions are publishers/libraries are taking to address the challenge?

I know that libraries are gradually getting more active within BISG, which is an interesting cross-pollination and puts them directly in touch with publishers. Publishers have a troubled recent history with libraries. Many are quite supportive but several have made some high-profile decisions around ebooks and other digital issues that have been met with dismay in the library community. I don't want to say, "it's early days" anymore — it's not — but most publishers have traditionally taken a while to feel comfortable with technology and I don't expect that to change drastically anytime soon.

If you could choose a first-priority action needed, what would it be?

Understanding search. And I think libraries are way ahead on this. Publishers need to understand that their books will be ingested wholesale into search engines and if they value what they publish, they will figure out how search engines work and mark up their books in ways that point searchers to them.

What outcomes would you like to see over the next 3-5 years?

This is hard to say. I think I'd like metadata to be used more in the form of semantic markup of ebook files so that it can be more valuable in organic search results. Why should a book be less searchable than a website, particularly when it's produced in XHTML?

Chapter 16: Thoughts on the Future of Publishing and Metadata

In an increasingly digital marketplace, it's become impossible to ignore the extent to which metadata is entangled with products — both physical and digital. In the virtual marketplace, the metadata that accompanies books represents the intellectual and business expertise that goes into creating, publishing, and marketing a book.

To quote Bill Kasdorf's comments from the previous chapter: *"Every year, the importance of metadata becomes clearer and clearer throughout the publishing ecosystem."*

We end the Handbook with the authors' views on the future of publishing and metadata. Following are our thoughts and updated responses to the questions we asked industry representatives.

Renée Register

Second Edition Update

For this edition, I'm adding my top five observations on today's publishing industry metadata landscape.

- Publishers want to do it for themselves. More publishers are implementing a direct to consumer option, highlighting the need for publishers to create and control their own metadata and increasing the importance of quality metadata at the beginning of the publishing lifecycle.
- Increasing adoption of identifier systems such as International Standard Name Identifier (ISNI) and International Standard Text Code (ISTC) facilitate continued movement toward realizing the potential of linked data and the Semantic Web. This open model also has implications for traditional proprietary data silos across the industry.
- The development of and interest in Thema, a global subject classification scheme for books, is bringing publishing closer to an international subject scheme.
- Options for metadata in EPUB 3 and HTML 5 point to further potential for the use of metadata embedded in digital content and business opportunities for packaging and marketing content components.
- Continued exploration of schema.org also opens up the ability to associate metadata with ever more granular content components and increases potential for discovery.

What is the most important metadata challenge facing publishers/libraries today?

Second Edition Update

The responses below remain relevant, but I'm adding what I believe to be a related imperative. Publishers must fully integrate 21st century metadata best practices and standards into their workflow, taking "ownership" of their metadata throughout its lifecycle.

This doesn't solve the problem of multiple metadata repositories that may contain differing versions of metadata for the same title. But the creation of complete, high quality metadata at the publisher level can reduce the need for downstream changes and create efficiencies in the supply chain.

Original First Edition Response

I'm listing two because they intersect on many levels.

- The sheer volume of metadata currently distributed via multiple data streams and stored in multiple repositories.
- The economics of metadata in current business models.

The management of rapidly expanding metadata volume, along with the growing number of metadata producers, is a major challenge. This is related to the increasing number of titles published each year in multiple formats. At the same time, and despite a countering trend toward open data, repositories of proprietary title data seem to be increasing rather than decreasing. This certainly reinforces the fact that metadata is powerful and a valuable business asset, but it inhibits the industry's ability to leverage metadata in ways that could create tremendous value and efficiencies.

It's important to remember that the title metadata (as opposed to business data that may need to be proprietary) held in these repositories references the same pool of titles available for sale from multiple vendors. Many versions of metadata referencing the same titles are held across multiple databases in various data formats — library records in MARC format, for example.

Some of this metadata is available for reuse (usually at a price) and some is not. The amount of money spent on collecting, refining, enhancing, and maintaining metadata for use in various systems and platforms, even when it's not repackaged and sold as a product, indicates its value as an asset in and of itself. The challenge is compounded by the fact that solutions may themselves pose a challenge to some current business models.

What actions are publishers/libraries are taking to address the challenge?

Second Edition Update

In the past few years, there has been a remarkable increase in publisher attention to metadata. Publishing organizations such as BISG and Digital Book World have responded by providing more training opportunities and resources in support of publishers.

Metadata silos and duplication of effort across the publishing industry and between publishers and libraries continue to be an issue. However, both communities show willingness to further explore the potential of identifiers and linked data to connect metadata across multiple formats and platforms.

Original First Edition Response

Publisher attention to metadata as an asset and understanding of the relationship of metadata to discovery and sales appears to be increasing. Attention to metadata upstream, at the publisher level, raises overall metadata quality, efficiency, and effectiveness throughout the supply chain and in the marketplace.

The library community is now exploring ways in which rich library stores of metadata can be released from MARC silos for use outside traditional library systems. This is a huge pool of expert-created, quality controlled metadata for the same titles represented in publishing industry databases. Moving away from silos created by data format also opens up potential for library use of publisher metadata.

In the broader world of metadata structures and uses, the movement toward open data, linked data, and the semantic web has huge implications for better use of publisher and library metadata.

If you could choose a first-priority action needed, what would it be?

Second Edition Update

I continue to see the search for "whole industry" solutions as a first-priority action.

Original First Edition Response

Face up to and address the problems head-on as an industry. This is one of the issues affecting the future of publishing and business models may have to change for the industry to move forward. More and more proprietary or in-house solutions will not fix the problem. Rejecting potential solutions because they also help competitors will not work in the long run. The industry should engage data and information experts outside of the industry to look at the overall problem in a much broader context. This applies to the library world as well.

What outcomes would you like to see over the next 3-5 years?

Second Edition Update

Although there is significant progress in the quality of publisher metadata and understanding of its dynamic nature, I continue to hope for continued action toward achieving the outcomes below.

Original First Edition Response

- Upstream publisher metadata is good enough and is updated frequently enough to greatly reduce the need for downstream modification or enhancement.
- The dynamic nature of metadata is embraced and metadata processes are an ongoing part of publishing workflow.
- Libraries are integrated into the downstream flow of metadata from publishers and libraries have ways to make full use of the metadata.
- Downstream metadata enhancements (from libraries and other suppliers) can easily move back upstream to benefit publishers.
- There is significant progress toward open data supporting concepts such as linked data.
- Shared technology, tools, and databases benefit multiple players.
- Libraries and publishers widely adopt shared standards and quality measures resulting in metadata than can be used and reused in multiple ways by multiple players.

Thad McIlroy

Second Edition Update

Below are Thad's updated responses to the questions.

....

What is the most important metadata challenge facing publishers today?

As the information in this book reveals, the practice of metadata has evolved significantly over the last several years. ONIX 3.0 has gone from a looming revised standard to a "must use" for serious publishers.

On the other hand, practices for accepting metadata are still sadly inconsistent; making it a problem for publishers to know which ONIX structure is required. When inconsistency is layered onto an already complex problem the situation approaches chaos.

Publishers need to really knuckle down on metadata, to understand the latest developments from the standards bodies and then the practical application of those standards.

What actions are publishers/libraries taking to address the challenge?

The largest publishers have the resources to assign dedicated personnel to address the challenges outlined above. Smaller publishers are often best served by specialized metadata service vendors such as Firebrand Technologies, Ingram, or BookNet in Canada and GiantChair in the UK.

If you could choose a first-priority action needed, what would it be?

The best way for a publisher to get a handle on metadata practices is to start with a single title and see it through all of the stages from production (both print and digital) right through to uploading the digital files for sales on all of the major etailers. The practice of metadata makes clear the theory of metadata.

What outcomes would you like to see over the next 3-5 years?

I hope that we can get all the "professional" publishers fully on the metadata program by then (by "professional publisher" I mean the companies that derive most of their income from publishing, or in the case of associations, have fully developed publishing programs).

The information needed to succeed is available and Digital Book World and other organizations offer ongoing professional training and certification.

I'll be pleased if in three-to-five years publishers understand sufficiently the hows and whys of metadata such that it becomes a routine part of their publishing workflow.

Thank You!

We hope you have found **The Metadata Handbook** *to be a helpful resource for learning about metadata in the publishing industry. We encourage you to explore the resources in the* **Bibliography and References** *section for use in your organizations. We welcome input and dialogue about the topics covered in the book. Our contact information can be found in the* **About the Authors** *section at the end of the book.*

Glossary

Algorithm
An algorithm is a set of instructions for performing a specific task and the action of algorithms on data structures is a basic part of modern computer science. Search engines (including bookseller search engines performing actions on book metadata) build proprietary algorithms designed to display the most relevant results from user searches acting on the available data. This could include keyword search results, a selection of books with similar categories, with the same author, or aimed at a certain age level. The algorithms determine which results are displayed and the order in which they are displayed. They accept, reject, and order results based on the set of instructions set by the search engine developers. Book metadata works behind the scenes as online retailers employ algorithms to present titles to users based on combinations of product metadata, search terms used, user history, sales history, and other variables. An algorithm may include instructions to reject certain results if analysis of the metadata detects practices designed to "trick" the system into providing results that aren't truly relevant. See also *Search Engine Optimization.*

Amazon Standard Identification Number (ASIN)
ASINs are proprietary numbers assigned by Amazon to each product sold on its sites. For books with 10-digit ISBNs, the ASIN and the ISBN are the same. Books without a 10-digit ISBN (books published before 1970 with no ISBN and books published after 2007 with a 13-digit ISBN only) are assigned unique ASINs, as are other Amazon non-book products. One ASIN refers only to one product but the same product may be referred to by several ASINs, and different Amazon national sites may use a different ASIN for the same product. Unless identical to the ISBN, Amazon book ASINs are not valid outside of the Amazon buying and selling environment. See also *Identifier; ISBN; SKU.*

American National Standards Institute (ANSI)
ANSI facilitates the development of American National Standards by accrediting the procedures of standards developing organizations, such as NISO. ANSI is the sole U.S. representative of the International Organization for Standardization (ISO). See also *International Organization for Standardization (ISO); National Information Standards Organization (NISO).*

ASIN. See *Amazon Standard Identification Number (ASIN).*

Barcode
A barcode is an optical machine-readable representation of data. The Bookland EAN is the most widely used international barcode format for publishing, and encodes the ISBN and price. The Bookland EAN barcode is required for print books by many book retailers and wholesalers and is used for automated tracking of sales information and inventory control. See also *Identifier; ISBN; SKU.*

BIC. See Book Industry Communication (BIC).

BISAC Subject Headings

BISAC Subject Headings are the North American standard for categorizing books based on topical content or genre. They help determine where physical books are shelved and are very important for online bookselling in metadata organization and search. Bookseller databases use them to create lists of titles by subject and in algorithms that suggest similar titles to readers. Most North American booksellers require publishers to supply at least one BISAC Subject Heading in each title record.

Here are a few examples of how they are applied.

- Metadata for adult books about internet marketing should include the BISAC Subject Heading Business & Economics/E-Commerce/Internet Marketing

- Metadata for adult historical mysteries should include the heading FICTION/Mystery/Historical

- Metadata for juvenile books about the internet should include the heading JUVENILE NONFICTION/Computers/Internet.

Book Industry Communication (BIC)

BIC is a UK-based membership organization supporting the book publishing industry and libraries. Among other services, the organization provides guidelines for implementing metadata and technical standards and best practices, maintains BIC Standard Subject Categories, and manages industry accreditation schemes. See also *Book Industry Study Group (BISG); BookNet Canada.*

Book Industry Study Group (BISG)

BISG is an American, not-for-profit membership organization that supports the book publishing industry through the development of standards, best practices, research, and events. BookNet Canada performs a similar role in that country. BISG and BookNet Canada also administer Metadata Certification programs. These programs evaluate the quality of a publisher's or vendor's metadata files based on structure, content, and adherence to best practices. Compliance to industry standards is evaluated and ranked by expert advisers and results in the awarding of levels of certification that may be shared with trading partners to indicate proficiency in metadata creation and adherence to standards. See also *Book Industry Communication (BIC); BookNet Canada.*

BookNet Canada

BookNet Canada is a non-profit organization that develops and supports technology, standards, and education for the Canadian Book Industry. See also *Book Information Communication (BIC); Book Industry Study Group (BISG).*

BISG. *See Book Industry Study Group (BISG).*

Check Digit

A check digit is used for error detection in automated processing of ISBNs. It consists of a single digit at the end of the ISBN calculated from the other digits in the ISBN. See also *ISBN.*

Cataloging in Publication (CIP)

Library of Congress, British Library, and Canadian CIP (Cataloging in Publication) programs were created to aid libraries by cataloging books in advance of publication. The publisher then includes printed CIP information on the copyright page of published books. CIP records are also distributed in electronic form to large libraries and subscribing vendors. With cataloging already available at the time of publication, books can be processed more efficiently and thus made available to library patrons more quickly. The CIP programs do not attempt to catalog every forthcoming publication and define some limitations in the scope of the programs. For example, self-published and print-on-demand publications are not eligible for the Library of Congress CIP program.

CIP. See *Cataloging in Publication (CIP)*.

Classification

Classification is categorization and organization based on shared qualities or characteristics. In book metadata, this involves categorizing books using defined codes or subject lists (controlled vocabularies) to describe a book's content. BISAC Subject Headings are the North American publishing industry standard for classifying books. Other widely adopted systems for classifying books include Dewey Decimal Classification, Library of Congress Classification, and Library of Congress Subject Headings in libraries, and BIC Standard Subject Categories in the UK publishing industry. See also *BIC Standard Subject Categories; BISAC Subject Headings; Controlled Vocabularies, Dewey Decimal Classification; Library of Congress Classification; Library of Congress Subject Headings; Taxonomy*.

Controlled Vocabulary

A controlled vocabulary is a selected list of words and phrases used to reduce ambiguity and ensure consistency in description. BISAC Subject Headings and ONIX Code Lists are examples of controlled vocabularies. Controlled vocabularies also provide consistency in interpretation of metadata transmitted and processed electronically. Words and phrases may also be represented by codes that further reduce error in machine interpretation. For example, the BISAC Subject Headings are also represented by codes, such as BUS090010, which has a literal translation of *BUSINESS and ECONOMICS/ E-Commerce/Internet Marketing*. The ONIX Contributor Code A01 indicates that the contributor name provided is the author of the book. Other codes indicate, editor, illustrator, and other contributor roles. Controlled vocabularies make it more likely that someone seeking information will retrieve a relevant set of items in a search. See also *Taxonomy*.

Data Aggregator

In the publishing industry, data aggregators collect, organize, and distribute book data from a variety of publishers, vendors, and other data suppliers in order to build a comprehensive catalog of product information. Data aggregators typically license their catalogs to libraries, retailers, and other data recipients. Examples include Bowker, based in the U.S., and UK-based Nielsen Book.

Dewy Decimal Classification

Dewey Decimal Classification is a system for coordinating library materials by subject. In libraries using the system, a "call number" derived from the assigned Dewey number is printed on the spine label affixed to printed books and used for library shelving organization. It was created by Melvil Dewey in 1876 and is used in more than 200,000 libraries around the world. OCLC owns the trademark and copyrights associated with Dewey Decimal Classification. See also *Classification*.

Digital Object Identifier (DOI)

DOI is a standard for identifying online content. A digital object is assigned a unique alphanumeric identifier accompanied by metadata describing the content. The DOI is permanent, allowing a digital object to be found even if the URL changes. Governed by the International DOI Foundation and administered by registration agencies, DOIs were initially developed to help protect the copyright of materials published on the internet. See also *Identifiers*.

Digital Rights Management (DRM)

The term DRM is broadly used to indicate digital technology appended to a digital file to restrict unauthorized access or track improper use. See also *Rights Management*.

Distributor

Book distributors act as a link between publishers and retailers. Although distributors do facilitate sales to retailers and libraries, publishers are their customers and distributors specifically represent publisher interests and activities. Their role may include receiving, displaying, and distributing publisher metadata. Distributors may specialize in a particular type of publisher — small, independent, or regional, for example — or they may specialize in publishers of certain types or genres of books, such as graphic novels or crafts books.

Document Type Definition (DTD)

A DTD is a formal description of the elements and markup tags allowable in a particular SGML, XML, or HTML document and where they can occur within the document. ONIX for Books download options include a DTD document. See also *Schema*.

DOI. See *Digital Objects Identifier (DOI)*.

DRM. See *Digital Rights Management (DRM)*.

DTD. See *Document Type Definition (DTD)*.

Dublin Core

Dublin Core grew out of 1995 meeting held at the library organization OCLC, located in Dublin, Ohio, to explore the creation of a core data set for describing Web-based resources. The resulting simple Dublin Core Metadata Element Set (DCMES) consists of fifteen elements. The EPUB standard uses DCMES to express electronic publication metadata. See also *EPUB*.

Ebook aggregator

The term "ebook aggregator" usually refers to a category of vendors providing ebooks and other electronic resources from multiple publishers, most commonly to libraries. These companies do not generally distribute into the retail market. Some are divisions of larger wholesalers or vendors. Examples include Overdrive, ebrary (a Proquest company), and MyiLibrary (owned by Ingram).

Ebook conversion

Most ebook digital files are converted from another data format, such as Adobe PDF or InDesign files. The process of conversion involves transformations and quality control steps to ensure that all of the formatted text appears accurately in the ebook file.

Ebook distributor

In this Handbook, ebook distributors are largely distinguished from ebook aggregators as vendors distributing directly into the retail market. Distribution into retail outlets such as Apple, Amazon, and Barnes & Noble is often offered along with ebook production and/ or conversion services, and distribution vendors may also support direct-to-consumer sales from their websites. See also *Ebook conversion*.

Ebook Format

Ebook formats allow display and navigation on reading devices and platforms that aren't possible using standard formats such as the Microsoft Document Format (.doc). Common examples include EPUB, KF8 (for Kindle), MOBI, and PDF. See also *EPUB; Kindle Format 8 (KF8); MOBI*.

EDI. See *Electronic Data Interchange (EDI)*.

EDItEUR

EDItEUR is the international group coordinating development of the ONIX standards for books, ebooks, and serials. They provide free ONIX documentation and support for ONIX implementation. They also maintain the EDIFACT and EDItX standards used for electronic communication of business-to-business transaction information. See also *Electronic Data Exchange (EDI); ONIX*.

Electronic Data Interchange (EDI)

EDI is a broad term for the online exchange of structured data relating to commerce. EDI standards, such as EDIFACT and EDItX, were developed to carry information regarding commercial transactions. They were not designed to carry product metadata with the fullness and form suitable for public display that can be carried in ONIX. EDIFACT or EDItX are used when the information supplied is for business-to-business transactions only and not intended for display to the public as descriptive information about a book. See also *ONIX*.

Enhanced Metadata

Metadata provided in addition to basic industry-recommended metadata elements is often referred to as enhanced metadata. This group of metadata elements includes information not strictly necessary for describing the book. Examples include reviews, author biographies and interviews, and tables of contents. It is also sometimes called "evaluative metadata" as it goes beyond basic description, providing additional information to help customers to evaluate the book's suitability for their needs.

EPUB

EPUB is a free and open standard file format for ebooks, developed and maintained by the International Digital Publishing Forum (IDPF). As an "open" standard, it is compatible with a wide range of ereaders as opposed to a "closed" or proprietary format that restricts use to a particular type of e-reader. The latest version, EPUB 3, was released in 2011. See also *International Digital Publishing Forum*.

Global Trade Item Number (GTIN/GTIN-13)

GTIN is a universal product identifier system for products that are bought and sold in the marketplace. GTINs may be 8, 12, 13, or 14 digits long. The expansion of ISBN to a 13-digit system allowed it to merge with GTIN-13. All book and serial publications sold internationally are expected to carry GTIN-13. The expansion of the ISBN to thirteen digits created conformance to the GTIN-13 standard, making ISBN consistent with other non-book products.

GTIN. See *Global Trade Item Number (GTIN/GTIN-13)*.

HyperText Markup Language (HTML)

HTML is the predominant language used for website design and creates the form and appearance of a web page. The original tag set was derived from SGML (Standard Generalized Markup Language) and HTML was standardized by the W3C as HTML 4. HTML 5 includes specific functions for embedding graphics, audio, video, and interactive documents and so, along with CSS 3, is expected to support websites substantially more visually elaborate and interactive than is the custom today. See also *W3C*.

I

Identifier
In metadata, an identifier is a language-independent label that uniquely "names" an object within an identification scheme. Language-independent means that the identifier is a numeric or alphanumeric code (rather than a book title or a personal name, for example) that always refers to the same thing. Identification schemes define the rules for constructing the identifier, including how many characters it contains and what those characters stand for. ISBN, ISSN, ISNI, and ISTC are examples of standard, publishing industry- approved identifiers. The use of the ISBN in publishing, for example, allows accurate communication about a particular book product without needing to state the title, publisher, binding, price, and other version-specific information in every transaction. It helps ensure that the correct version of a book is delivered to the customer and that sales information is accurately captured. Individual vendors may assign proprietary identifiers (Amazon ASINs or vendor SKUs, for example) to their products, but these are useful only within the vendors' systems and are not internationally recognized or controlled. A proprietary product number should not take the place of an industry-approved standard identifier, although both numbers may certainly co-exist within a bookseller's system. Identifiers that are accepted and controlled globally are reliably recognized and interpreted across multiple systems and e-commerce sites.

IDPF. See *International Digital Publishing Forum (IDPF)*.

Imprint
A book publisher may have multiple imprints under which it publishes titles. Imprints have their own identity, marketing strategies, and metadata variations. They can be business units of publishing houses but are essentially "brands." The books published under an imprint may have a defining genre, subject, or character, such as mystery fiction, literary fiction, or business books. Examples include the Little, Brown imprint Mulholland Books (specializing in suspense) and Grand Central Publishing's Business Plus. An imprint could also be aimed at a particular audience, such as children or young adults (the HarperCollins imprint HarperTeen, for example), or could consist of books curated by a renowned editor or author, such as the Nan A. Talese imprint from Random House.

Independent Publisher
Independent publishers are those that are not part of a large publishing or media organization. Small publishers are often independent as well and the terms "small publisher" and "independent publisher" are sometimes used interchangeably. The Independent Publishers Group (IPG) distributes for many independent publishers and its website provides examples of publishers in this category.

International Digital Publishing Forum (IDPF)
IDPF is a global trade and standards organization for the development and promotion of electronic publishing. The IDPF develops and maintains the EPUB format. See also *EPUB*.

International Standard Book Number (ISBN)
ISBN is the ISO-approved global standard for identifying a book product. ISBN use facilitates commerce activities across countries and systems by providing a unique identifier that always refers to the same product. The identifier provides reliable and unambiguous machine matching to a specific version of a book for buying and selling activities. Since January

2007, all ISBNs issued conform to a 13-digit standard. The expansion increased capacity and also allowed ISBN to merge with the GTIN (Global Trade Identification Number) data structure. The GTIN family includes the UPC (Universal Product Code) that is used in creating machine-readable barcodes. The ISBN is now consistent with the international product identification system used by multiple industries to buy, sell, and track non-book products. See also *Identifier; ISO; UPC.*

International Standard Name Identifier (ISNI)

The 16-digit ISNI is an ISO standard for the identification of "Public Identities." ISNIs are assigned to the "Public Identities" of parties that participate in the creation, production, management or distribution of cultural goods. The party can be a person, such as a book author, or a legal entity, such as a record label. It provides a tool for pulling together different forms of a name (such as linking pseudonyms to the appropriate identity), or to disambiguate multiple identities with the same name (John Smith, for example). Consistent use of ISNI as part of book metadata about contributor names would make it much easier for bookseller sites to correctly display all titles by the same author, even if the author's name is identical or similar to many other author names. See also *Identifiers; ISO.*

International Standard Text Code (ISTC)

The ISTC, a numbering system to uniquely identify text-based works, was published as an ISO (see below) standard in 2009. Unlike the ISBN, the ISTC identifies a "work" rather than a "product" and allows linking together of publications with the same basic content. For example, *Sense and Sensibility* is a "work" that is available as many different "products" that are packaged in many formats (paperback, hardcover, ebook, etc.) by various publishers. Each of these products should have a unique ISBN but should carry the same ISTC, allowing the entire range of choices to be easily retrieved and displayed to consumers on bookseller websites. See also *Identifiers; ISO.*

International Organization of Standards (ISO)

ISO is an independent, non-governmental organization founded in 1947 "to facilitate the international coordination and unification of industrial standards." It the largest developer of voluntary international standards and the organization has published more than 19,000 international standards covering most aspects of technology and business. Organizational membership is made up of national standards bodies in approximately 130 countries. ISO-approved standards, such as ISBN, have been developed and tested by an expert technical committee consensus process to ensure their efficacy for international business transactions. When a standard has been ISO-approved, industries have assurance that when they provide electronic information conforming to the standard it will be consistently received and understood by business partners worldwide.

International Standard Serial Number (ISSN)

A unique 8-digit code, ISSN is the international identifier for print and electronic serial publications such as newspapers, magazines, and other continuing resource of all kinds. As opposed to stand-alone books (monographs), serials are issued on a regular basis and have the same title (The New York Times, for example) but different content. The ISSN allows all the different issues of a serial publication to be reliably tracked, retrieved and displayed. The ISSN International Centre was created in Paris in 1976 under the terms of an agreement between UNESCO and France, the host country. The ISSN International Centre coordinates the ISSN assignment and management activities of 88 member countries. See also *Identifiers.*

ISBN. See *International Standard Book Number (ISBN)*.

ISBN Agency
ISBN Agencies are established on a country-by-country basis in coordination with the International ISBN Agency (IIA). Publishers obtain ISBNs from the appropriate national agency, based on their primary location of operation. Fee structures are determined by the individual ISBN agencies. Bowker is the official U.S. ISBN agency, and Nielsen is the UK agency, while the Canadian ISBN Service System (CISS) (in French, le Système de service canadien de l'ISBN (SSCI)) is operated by Library and Archives Canada.

ISNI. See *International Standard Name Identifier (ISNI)*.

ISO. See *International Organization of Standards. (ISO)*.

ISTC. See *International Standard Text Code (ISTC)*.

ISSN. See *International Standard Serial Number (ISSN)*.

Keyword
Keywords and phrases are free-text terms included in metadata to supplement description of content and provide search terms that might assist in search engine optimization. Keywords are not a substitute for the application of controlled subject vocabularies, such as BISAC Subject Headings, and should not duplicate terms found elsewhere in the metadata. See also *BISAC Subject Headings*.

Kindle Format 8 (KF8)
Amazon's Kindle Format 8 largely emulates the functionality of the EPUB format, but is proprietary to Amazon and is designed to work only with Amazon devices and apps. The Kindle Gen tool is used to convert files to the Kindle Format. See also *EPUB 3*.

LCCN. See *Library of Congress Control Number (LCCN)*.

Library of Congress Control Number (LCCN)
The LCCN is a unique number assigned by the Library of Congress and used to identify a bibliographic record corresponding to a publication. It is not used for commercial product identification purposes (the ISBN is used for this purpose) but provides a reliable match point to retrieve a record in the Library of Congress database and other library databases. An LCCN may be assigned pre-publication through the Preassigned Control Number Program (PCN). Once assigned, it's commonly printed inside the book. See also *International Standard Book Number (ISBN)*.

Linked Data
Linked data refers to a way of connecting related data on the Web through linking pieces of data across the current silos created by individual web pages and discrete databases. It is closely associated with the concept of a "semantic web" and is built on W3C Resource Data Framework (RDF) specifications. See also *RDF; Semantic Web; W3C*.

MARC (Machine Readable Cataloging)
The library community developed the MARC (MAchine Readable Cataloging) record format in the late 1960s to allow electronic exchange and online display of data traditionally shown in card catalogs. Most library catalog records are still stored and shared in MARC format. MARC-21 is the most commonly used version of MARC.

Metadata

Although metadata is often defined as "data about data," we don't usually think of books, movies, and other forms of artistic or intellectual content as "data." Some forms of metadata do provide structural information about *carriers* of data (an ONIX file for example) or *containers* of data, such as a webpage or an ebook. Although metadata carriers and containers are discussed in this *Handbook*, it is strongly focused on metadata that describes a book's content, format, and terms of sale for the purposes of discovery, access, and business processes related to publishing and bookselling. Information about books (title, author, publisher, price, etc.) may be distributed (carried) in an ONIX or Excel file and displayed (contained) on a webpage or within an ebook, but metadata is the actual information that is carried or contained. See also *Metadata Carrier; Ebook Format*.

Metadata Best Practices

A best practice is a technique or method that consistently shows superior results and that is therefore used as an industry benchmark. Adoption of best practices is generally voluntary, but is encouraged by industries to promote efficiency and consistency in business and technology practices across multiple participants, systems, and business transactions. The North American publishing industry looks to Best Practices for Product Metadata, developed by the BISG Metadata Committee in coordination with BookNet Canada, for book metadata guidelines and recommendations. See also *Book Industry Study Group (BISG)*.

Metadata Element

As used in this book, a metadata element is a defined and structured piece of information about a book: title, contributor, publisher, publication date, etc. Within an ONIX record or other metadata carrier, an element may need to be expressed by using more than one field. For example, a contributor could include a first name, last name, and title, and all contributors are accompanied by a role code, such as author, illustrator, or editor.

Metadata Carrier

A metadata carrier is the structured format by which metadata is distributed electronically for use by multiple receivers, in this case book metadata for the publishing industry. The metadata in electronic files, composed of book records, is structured in a way that allows consistent interpretation and display across many different systems. XML-based ONIX for Books is the international standard for carrying book metadata. See also *ONIX; XML (Extensible Mark-Up Language)*.

Metadata Distribution

In the publishing industry (and for products in many other industries) product metadata is distributed separately from the product itself. It is often distributed well in advance of product availability and can be used as a selection tool for booksellers and libraries as well as to populate online bookselling sites, providing the information seen by consumers. Metadata may be communicated by publishers, wholesalers, distributors, and by metadata aggregators whose role is to collect and disseminate information about millions of books from multiple publishers.

Meta Tags

Meta tags are used in web page authoring to include additional information about the content of the page, such as page description, keywords, and author to be used by web browsers, search engines, and other web applications. The meta element is defined within the W3C specifications.

MOBI
MOBI is the ebook format developed for the MobiPocket Reader. See also *Ebook File Format*.

Monograph
In bibliographic terms, a monograph is a publication that is either complete in one part, a stand-alone book, or complete in a finite number of separate parts. See also *Serial*.

National Information Standards Organization (NISO)
A non-profit association accredited by the American National Standards Institute (ANSI), NISO identifies, develops, maintains, and publishes technical standards to manage information. NISO standards apply both traditional and new technologies to the full range of information-related needs, including retrieval, re-purposing, storage, metadata, and preservation. See also *American National Standards Institute (ANSI)*.

NISO. See *National Information Standards Organization (NISO)*.

ONIX
The ONIX family includes XML-based standards for Books, Serials, and Licensing Terms & Rights Information. These standards support efficient and reliable computer-to-computer communication between publishing industry participants such as publishers, wholesalers, and retailers. ONIX for Books is the international standard for electronic communication of book industry product information. EDItEUR coordinates development of ONIX standards. See also *EDiTEUR; XML (Extensible Mark-Up Language)*.

On Sale Date
This is the date specified by the publisher on which a book, usually a new release title, offered for the first time, may legally be sold to consumers. It is a binding legal contract between publishers and retailers that the retailer will not sell any copies of the book before that date. In recent years, for example, on sale date was applied, and compliance strictly enforced, for major titles, such as Harry Potter or Oprah Book Club titles. Suppliers may be required to sign an affidavit in order to receive the title before on sale date. BISG's *On Sale Date Compliance: Recommended Best Practices* recommends that on sale date be applied to every new release title and that a general affidavit, rather than title-specific affidavits, be used. On sale date is not the same as the publication date. Publishers should communicate each date in the appropriate ONIX field. See also *Publication Date*.

PDF
An abbreviation for Portable Document Format, PDF files were invented and championed by Adobe Systems with its Acrobat software. PDF files represent documents independently of the software, hardware, and operating system used to create them. Adobe turned control of the format over to ISO, the International Organization for Standardization, where on July 1, 2008 it was published as ISO 32000-1:2008.

Print on Demand (POD)
Print on demand combines fast and economical digital printing technology with a business model that prints publications at the time of order rather than determining print run quantities in advance of publication. POD generated new publishing opportunities (for self-publishing and publishing of public domain works) and services such as Ingram's Lightning Source and Amazon's CreateSpace.

Publication Date

For marketing and metadata purposes, the publication date begins as the date the publisher plans to publish the book. This date is communicated in product metadata feeds and displayed on websites long before the planned publication date and may change during production and the metadata lifecycle. Publishers should send updates to supplier metadata when the planned publication date changes. The final date (usually the year of publication only) appears on the title page verso (the page following the title page) of the published book. Publication date is not the same as copyright date or on sale date. See also *Copyright Date; On Sale Date.*

Publisher Supply Chain

Supply chain participants and activities move a product from the supplier to the consumer. In publishing, the supply chain includes wholesalers, distributors, data and content aggregators, retailers, and libraries. The publisher is generally the initial supplier and the published product moves through various channels to the consumer. In self-publishing, the author is also the supplier and so usually interacts with supply chain participants in order to reach consumers. See also *Supply Chain.*

RDF. See *Resource Description Framework (RDF).*

Resource Description Framework (RDF)

RDF is a W3C standard defining metadata structures about Web resources so the data can be exchanged between applications without loss of meaning. RDF is a major component in Semantic Web activities. See also *Semantic Web; W3C.*

Schema

In data, a schema is generally a document defining data relationships. An XML schema describes the relationship and attributes of data elements in some other class of XML document. ONIX for Books download options include an XML schema. See also *DTD.*

Schema.org

Schema.org is a collection of schemas used to markup HTML pages in ways that are recognized by major search engines and improve the display of search results. On-page markup enables search engines to understand the information on web pages and provide richer search results making it easier for users to find relevant information.

Search Engine Optimization (SEO)

Search engines rank and display search results based on algorithms designed to determine which sites and pages are most relevant to the user's search. SEO is an increasingly formal set of practices, often performed by trained and experienced professionals, designed to make a web site not only findable by search engines, but with a high relevancy ranking resulting in display near the top of search results. Search engine developers continually study and revise search algorithms to increase relevancy and thwart attempts to game the system so keeping up is a moving target. Metadata that fully and accurately describes content contributes to search engine optimization and is one factor that publishers can control and monitor.

Self-publisher

A self-publisher is an author who undertakes the editorial, production, marketing, and distribution tasks associated with traditional book publication.

Semantic Web

In a 2009 TED Talk, Tim Berners-Lee introduced the concept of a "Semantic Web" to the general public. A Semantic Web would allow linking of data across web pages and data silos. Web search engine results now consist of hyperlinks to HTML documents but the raw data itself isn't available. Using the concept of linked data, a Semantic Web model would allow the Web to be treated and researched as if it were one database, pulling together relevant results from multiple sources. See also *Linked data.*

SEO. See *Search Engine Optimization (SEO).*

Serial

A serial publication is issued in discrete parts (usually numbered or dated) and intended to continue indefinitely. New parts may be issued at regular or irregular intervals and may be priced as individual volumes or on a subscription basis. "Serial" is often used interchangeably with "periodical" but "periodical" has a specific meaning. A periodical has a distinctive title and is issued more than once a year, with each issue containing articles by several contributors. See also *Monograph.*

SAN. See *Standard Address Number (SAN).*

SKU. See *Stock Keeping Unit (SKU).*

Standard

A standard is an accepted norm related to the operation of technical systems. Standards are often developed and issued by a trade association representing an industry or technology segment and adopted by national or international standards organizations. ISBN, ONIX, and EPUB are examples of standards. See also *International Organization of Standards (ISO).*

Standard Address Number (SAN)

The SAN is a unique seven-digit identifier signifying addresses of organizations involved in the publishing industry. SANs are used in electronic communications to accurately identify participants in commercial transactions.

Stock Keeping Unit (SKU)

SKU is a number or code used to identify each distinct product or service for sale, allowing businesses to track inventory and product availability. SKUs are often used to refer to different versions of the same product. Unlike ISBN and other nationally and internationally standardized identifiers, SKUs are usually assigned at the merchant level.

Strict-On-Sale (SOS) date. See *On Sale Date.*

Structured Data

Structured data resides in fixed fields within a record or file. The metadata in ONIX files and records is structured data. Although data in XML files are not fixed in location like traditional database records, they are nevertheless structured because the data are tagged and can be accurately identified. In contrast, unstructured data is generally free-form text such as that found in word processing documents, web pages, and email messages.

Supply Chain

Supply chain refers to the steps, processes, and entities (companies, organizations, or people) needed to get products and services to consumers. A supply chain involves multiple players such as suppliers, manufacturers, wholesalers, and retailers. See also *Publisher Supply Chain.*

Taxonomy

In metadata, a taxonomy is typically a type of controlled vocabulary that is structured hierarchically — the terms in the taxonomy have relationships to other terms. There are different types of hierarchy, but in general a broader "parent" term has narrower terms, or "children." In BISAC Subject Headings, for example, the broader term of Fiction has subcategories of Fiction—Historical, Fiction—Mystery, and so on. See also *Controlled Vocabulary*.

Territorial Rights
Territorial rights are the rights to sell a product in a specific geographical area. The right to sell may carry conditions that specific methods of selling are used. Territorial rights may specify a country, a group of countries, or worldwide rights. The same work may have different publishers holding different territorial rights. For example, a British publisher may sell a work's rights to a U.S. publisher with the condition that the U.S. publisher's version may only be sold in North America. ONIX 2.1 and 3.0 both allow detailed descriptions of territorial rights.

Thema
Thema is a global subject classification system for books, which is gathering wide international participation. Thema aims to reduce the duplication of effort in maintaining and applying multiple national subject schemes and the need for mapping between schemes. It can be used along with existing schemes, such as BISAC and BIC.

UPC. See *Universal Product Code (UPC, UPC-12)*.

Universal Product Code (UPC, UPC-12)
UPC is a unique numerical identifier for machine-readable encoding, currently used exclusively in barcodes. UPC is used mainly for media—music, movies, and video games, for example. ISBN is the required identifier encoded in book barcodes, but mass-market paperbacks may also carry a barcode encoded with UPC because they are commonly sold in outlets such as supermarkets, drugstores, and big-box chain stores.

Validation
In computer science and the metadata world, validation usually means "data validation" or "file validation." Data validation uses automated routines that check inbound or outbound data based on correctness, completeness, security, and other criteria. For example, most systems will not load an ISBN that does not have a valid "check digit" as this means the ISBN itself is not valid. Validation can be applied to a data element, such as the ISBN example, and to the entire file based on conformance to the file's schema. Most ONIX recipients run files through a validation program before loading. See also *Check-digit; Schema*.

W3C
W3C is an abbreviation for the World Wide Web Consortium, a very broad international group that develops consensus protocols and specifications to enhance the interoperability and functionality of the World Wide Web.

XML (Extensible Mark-Up Language)
XML was designed to structure, store, and transport data electronically, whereas HTML (Hypertext Markup Language) was designed to facilitate web-based display of information. XML was designed to promote usability over the internet and is the most common tool for data transmission between applications. For example, XML-based formats have become the default for many office productivity tools, such as Microsoft Word and Apple's iWork. Information carried in standards created using XML format, such as ONIX, can be understood by most business partners and systems involved in publishing and bookselling.

Bibliography & References

Books

Battles, Matthew. *Library: an unquiet history*. New York: W.W. Norton, 2003. Print and digital.

Blum, Andrew. *Tubes: a journey to the center of the Internet*. New York: Ecco, 2012. Print and digital.

Chandra, Vikram. *Geek sublime: the beauty of code, the code of beauty*. Minneapolis, Minn.: Graywolf Press, 2014. Print and digital.

Dyson, George. *Turing's cathedral: the origins of the digital universe*. New York: Pantheon Books, 2012. Print and digital.

Gleick, James. *The information: a history, a theory, a flood*. New York: Vintage, 2012. Print and digital.

Greenfield, Jeremy, Editor. *Finding the future of digital publishing: interviews with 19 innovative ebook business leaders*. New York: Digital Book World, 2012. Digital.

Isaacson, Walter. *The innovators: how a group of hackers, geniuses, and geeks created the digital revolution*. New York: Simon & Schuster, 2014. Print and digital.

Kaku, Michio. *Physics of the future: how science will shape human destiny and our daily lives by the year 2100*. New York: Anchor Books, 2012. Print and digital.

Lanier, Jaron. *You are not a gadget: a manifesto*. New York: Alfred A. Knopf, 2010. Print and digital.

Lanier, Jason. *Who owns the future?* New York: Simon & Schuster, 2014. Print, audio and digital.

Lyons, Martyn. *Books: a living history*. Los Angeles: J. Paul Getty Museum, 2011. Print.

MacCormick, John. *Nine algorithms that changed the future: the ingenious ideas that drive today's computers*. Princeton, N.J: Princeton University Press, 2012. Print and digital.

McGuire, Hugh, and Brian O'Leary. *Book: a futurist's manifesto: essays from the bleeding edge of publishing*. Boston, Mass: O'Reilly, 2012. Print and digital.

Mendelsund, Peter. *What we see when we read*. New York: Vintage, 2014. Print and digital.

Pinker, Steven. *The sense of style: the thinking person's guide to writing in the 21st century*. New York: Viking Books, 2014. Print and digital.

Rudder, Christian. *Dataclysm: who we are (when we think no one's looking)*. New York: Crown, 2014. Print and digital.

Rushkoff, Douglas. *Program or be programmed: ten commands for a digital age*. Berkeley, Calif.: Soft Skull Press, 2011. Print and digital.

Schmidt, Eric and Rosenberg, Jonathan. *How google works*. New York: Grand Central Publishing, 2014. Print, digital, and audio.

Schnapp, Jeffrey T. and Battles, Matthew. *The library beyond the book*. Cambridge, Mass.: Harvard University Press, 2014. Print.

Stone, Brad. *The everything store: Jeff Bezos and the age of Amazon*. New York: Little, Brown and Company, 2013.

Thompson, John B.. *Merchants of culture: the publishing business in the twenty-first century*. Second ed. New York, New York: Plume, 2012. Print.

Industry Reference

LMP: literary market place : the directory of the American book publishing industry with industry yellow pages. Medford, NJ: Information Today, Inc. Print and digital.

Books in print. New Providence, N.J.: R.R. Bowker Co., 0. Print and digital.

Kasdorf, William E.. *The Columbia guide to digital publishing*. New York: Columbia University Press, 2003. Print.

"U.S. Copyright Office - Definitions (FAQ)." U.S. Copyright Office.

Research and Reports

"BNC Research: The Canadian Book Market." *BookNet Canada*.

BookStats: a comprehensive study of the U.S. publishing industry. Association of American Publishers, Book Industry Study Group. New York: BISG. Published annually. Print and digital.

Coyle, Karen. Understanding the Semantic Web: Bibliographic Data and Metadata. Chicago, IL: ALA TechSource, 2010. Print.

"The Development, Use, and Modification of Book Product Metadata | Book Industry Study Group." *Book Industry Study Group*.

"The link between metadata and sales | Nielsen BookData." *Nielsen BookData*.

Metadata Standards, Best Practices, and Classification

Available from BookNet Canada - www.booknetcanada.ca

BNC Standards and Certification

The Canadian Book Market

The Canadian Book Consumer

Available from Book Industry Communication - www.bic.org.uk

Product Data Guidelines ONIX for Books Release 3

BIC Basic

BIC Standard Subject Categories

BIC Training

BIC Publications

Available from Book Industry Study Group - www.bisg.org

Product Metadata Best Practices

Best Practices for Keywords in Metadata

Recommendations for Citing Common Core State Standards in ONIX

BISAC Subject Headings

Recommended Best Practices for On Sale Date Compliance

ONIX Users Directory - Receivers

Product Data Certification Program

Available from EDItEUR - www.editeur.org

Release 3.0 Downloads

- Core documentation
- Best practice guidelines
- Schema definitions
- ONIX 3.0 tagname converter and Large file splitter
- Code Lists for Release 3.0
- How to describe sets and series in ONIX 3.0
- How to describe digital products in ONIX 3.0
- How to send block updates in ONIX 3.0
- How to specify different terms of supply in different territories

ONIX & MARC 21

Thema Subject Category Scheme

Identifiers

ISBN
"ISBN Users Manual." *International ISBN Agency.*

ISBN and Digital Resources
"Guidelines for Assignment to E-books." *International ISBN Agency.*

"BISG Policy Statement – 1101: Best Practices for Identifying Digital Products." *Book Industry Study Group.*

ISTC
"ISTC - International Standard Text Code." *ISTC - International Standard Text Code.*

"Frequently asked questions about ISTC." *Bowker Identifier Services.*

"About the ISTC." *Nielsen ISTC Agency.*

ISNI
ISNI Resources. *ISNI International Agency.*

EPUB

"BISG Policy Statement – 1201: Endorsement of EPUB 3." *Book Industry Study Group.*

"EPUB 3.0 Support Grid." *Book Industry Study Group.*

"EPUB Publications 3.0." *International Digital Publishing Forum.*

"AAP EPUB 3 Implementation White Paper." *International Digital Publishing Forum.*

Library Metadata

"Understanding MARC Bibliographic: Machine-Readable Cataloging." *Library of Congress.*

"A Bibliographic Framework for the Digital Age (October 31, 2011): Bibliographic Framework Transition Initiative (Library of Congress)." *Library of Congress.*

"International Standard Bibliographic Description | IFLA." *International Federation of Library Associations and Institutions (IFLA)*.

Resource description & access: RDA. Chicago, IL: American Library Association, 2011. Print.

"Joint Steering Committee for Development of RDA: A Brief History of AACR." *Joint Steering Committee for Development of RDA*.

"Dewey Decimal Classification Summaries." *OCLC*.

"Subject Headings - Cataloging and Acquisitions (Library of Congress)." *Library of Congress*.

"Library of Congress Classification Outline - Classification - Cataloging and Acquisitions (Library of Congress)." *Library of Congress*.

"A Crosswalk from ONIX Version 3.0 to MARC 21." *Jean Godby, OCLC Research*.

Linked Data and the Semantic Web

"Introducing Linked Data And The Semantic Web." *Linked Data Tools Free Downloads Semantic Web*.

"Semantic Web - W3C." *World Wide Web Consortium (W3C)*.

"Tim Berners-Lee on the next Web | Video on TED.com." *TED: Ideas worth spreading*.

The Linking Open Data Cloud Diagram. *Insight Center for Data Analytics*.

Linked Data Links. *Karen Coyle*.

Industry Organizations

United States

American Library Association
www.ala.org
ALA is the oldest and largest library association in the world. Services include association information, news, events, and advocacy resources for members.

American National Standards Institute (ANSI)
www.ansi.org
The American National Standards Institute (ANSI) has served in its capacity as administrator and coordinator of the United States private sector voluntary standardization system for more than ninety years. ANSI facilitates the development of American National Standards (ANS) by accrediting the procedures of standards developing organizations (SDOs).

Association of American Publishers (AAP)
www.publishers.org
AAP is the trade association for the U.S. book publishers, providing advocacy and communications on behalf of the industry.
- Trade
  www.publishers.org/trade
- Professional/Scholarly Publishing
  www.pspcentral.org
- Higher Education
  www.publishers.org/highered
- K-12 School
  www.publishers.org/school

Association of American University Presses (AAUP)
www.aaupnet.org
The AAUP is an organization of nonprofit publishers whose members strive to advance scholarship through their offerings. The Association's mission is to assist its members through professional education, cooperative services, and public advocacy. AAUP offers training programs and workshops, holds specialized and general annual meetings, and aggregates and distributes industry information.

American Booksellers Association (ABA)
www.bookweb.org
ABA is the national trade organization for independent booksellers.

Association of Educational Publishers (AEP)
www.aepweb.org
AEP is a professional organization serving the diverse needs of the entire educational resource community, the Association of Educational Publishers (AEP) encourages and advocates for professional, quality content for teaching and learning.

The Authors Guild
www.authorsguild.org
The Authors Guild has been the nation's leading advocate for writers' interests in effective copyright protection, fair contracts and free expression since it was founded as the Authors League of America in

1912. It provides legal assistance and a broad range of web services to its members.

Book Industry Study Group (BISG)
www.bisg.org
The Book Industry Study Group (BISG) is a national, not-for-profit U.S. book trade association with the mission of creating a more informed, empowered and efficient book industry.

Evangelical Christian Publishers Association (ECPA)
www.ecpa.org
The Evangelical Christian Publishers Association (ECPA) is an international non-profit trade organization comprised of member companies that are involved in the publishing and distribution of Christian content worldwide.

Independent Book Publishers Association (IBPA)
www.ibpa-online.org
The Independent Book Publishers Association is the largest not-for-profit trade association representing independent book publishers. Founded in 1983, it serves book publishers located in the United States and around the world.

International Digital Publishing Forum (IDPF)
www.idpf.org
The International Digital Publishing Forum (IDPF) is the global trade and standards organization dedicated to the development and promotion of electronic publishing and content consumption.

Library of Congress
www.loc.org
Of interest to publishers:

- **Cataloging in Publication Program (CIP)**
  www.loc.gov/publish/cip
  A Cataloging in Publication record (aka CIP data) is a bibliographic record prepared by the Library of Congress for a book that has not yet been published. When the book is published, the publisher includes the CIP data on the copyright page thereby facilitating book processing for libraries and book dealers.

- **Preassigned Control Number Program (PCN)**
  www.loc.gov/publish/pcn
  The purpose of the Preassigned Control Number (PCN) program is to enable the Library of Congress to assign control numbers in advance of publication to those titles that may be added to the Library's collections. A Library of Congress catalog control number is a unique identification number that the Library of Congress assigns to the catalog record created for each book in its cataloged collections.

National Association of College Stores (NACS)
www.nacs.org
The National Association of College Stores (NACS) is a not-for-profit trade association representing the $10 billion campus retailing industry. Membership includes more than 3,000 stores serving colleges, universities, and K-12 schools. NACS members also include higher education professionals, organizations, associations, and others interested in the industry's vitality.

National Information Standards Organization (NISO)
www.niso.org
NISO, a non-profit association accredited by the American National Standards Institute (ANSI), identifies, develops, maintains, and publishes technical standards to manage information in our changing and ever-more digital environment.

OCLC (Online Library Computer Center)
www.oclc.org
OCLC is a worldwide library cooperative. The organization maintains WorldCat, a database containing over two million bibliographic records and the hold-

ings of seventy-two thousand libraries worldwide. Of interest to publishers:

- OCLC Metadata Services for Publishers
- OCLC Contract Cataloging for Publishers
  www.publishers.oclc.org

PEN American Center
www.pen.org

PEN American Center is the U.S. branch of the world's oldest international literary and human rights organization. International PEN was founded in 1921 in direct response to the ethnic and national divisions that contributed to the First World War. PEN American Center was founded in 1922 and is the largest of the 144 PEN centers in 101 countries that together compose International PEN.

Small Publishers Association (SPAN)
www.spanpro.org

SPAN is a nonprofit trade association of authors and independent publishers with the mission of building successful writing and publishing businesses.

Society for Scholarly Publishing (SSP)
www.sspnet.org

SSP is a nonprofit organization formed to promote and advance communication among all sectors of the scholarly publication community through networking, information dissemination, and facilitation of new developments in the field.

Canada

Association of Canadian Publishers (ACP)
www.publishers.ca

The Association of Canadian Publishers (ACP) represents approximately 135 Canadian-owned and controlled book publishers from across the country.

Association of Canadian University Presses (ACUP) / Association Des Presses Universitaires Canadiennes (APUC)
www.acup.ca

The Association of Canadian University Presses / Association Des Presses Universitaires Canadiennes exists to serve the interest of Canadian scholarship. The ACUP / APUC is a source for publishing advice and assistance to learned bodies, scholarly associations, institutions of higher learning, and individual scholars and the major voice of the scholarly publishing community to government, to the media, and to the public.

BookNet Canada
www.booknetcanada.ca

BookNet Canada focuses on Bibliographic Data, Electronic Data Interchange (EDI), Sales Data Analysis, international standards, and the sourcing of other technologies and services to enhance publisher supply chain efficiencies.

Canadian Author's Association
www.canauthors.org

The Canadian Authors Association (CAA) is a national organization dedicated to promoting a flourishing community of writers across Canada and to encourage works of literary and artistic merit.

Canadian Library Association (CLA)
www.cla.ca

The Canadian Library Association / Association canadienne des bibliothèques was founded in Hamilton, Ontario in 1946, and was incorporated under the Companies Act on November 26, 1947. CLA is a non-profit voluntary organization, governed by an elected Executive Council, which is advised by over thirty interest groups and committees.

Canadian Publisher's Council (CPC)

www.pubcouncil.ca

The Canadian Publishers' Council is Canada's main English language book publishing trade association and represents the interests of publishing companies that publish books and other media for elementary and secondary schools, colleges and universities, professional and reference markets, the retail and library sectors. Members employ more than 2800 Canadians and collectively account for nearly three-quarters of all domestic sales of English-language books.

Library and Archives Canada

www.collectionscanada.gc.ca

Of interest to publishers:

- **ISBN Agency**
  Library and Archives Canada serves as the National ISBN Agency. The Library also issues International Standard Serial Number (ISSN) and International Standard Music Number (ISMN) identifiers.

- **Cataloguing in Publication (CIP)**
  Cataloguing in Publication (CIP) is a voluntary program of cooperation between publishers and libraries. It enables the cataloguing of books BEFORE they are published, and the prompt distribution of this cataloging information to booksellers and libraries. The Canadian CIP Program is coordinated by Library and Archives Canada.

Standards Council of Canada (SCC)

www.scc.ca

The Standards Council of Canada (SCC) is a federal Crown corporation. Its mandate to promote efficient and effective standardization in Canada. The organization oversees Canada's National Standards System.

Writers Union of Canada

www.writersunion.ca

The Writers' Union of Canada is the national organization of professional writers of books. Now 1,900 members strong, the Union was founded more than thirty-five years ago to work with governments, publishers, booksellers, and readers to improve the conditions of Canadian writers.

United Kingdom

Book Industry Communication (BIC)

www.bic.org.uk

BIC is an independent organization set up and sponsored by the Publishers Association, Booksellers Association, the Chartered Institute of Library and Information Professionals, and the British Library to promote supply chain efficiency in all sectors of the book world through e-commerce and the application of standard processes and procedures.

Booksellers Association (BA)

www.booksellers.org.uk

The Booksellers Association is a membership organization for all booksellers in the UK & Ireland, and represents more than 95% of booksellers. The BA represents and promotes its membership and provides a full range of products and services to members.

British Library

www.bl.uk

Of interest to publishers:

Publishers and distributors in the United Kingdom and the Republic of Ireland have a legal obligation to send one copy of each of their publications to the Legal Deposit Office of the British Library within one month of publication.

British Standards Institute (BSI)
www.bsigroup.com
BSI Standards is the UK's National Standards Body.

Chartered Institute of Library and Information Professionals (CILIP)
www.clip.org.uk
CILIP is a membership organization for library and information professionals, providing professional services, external relations, and resources.

Independent Publishers Guild (IPG)
www.ipg.uk.com
IPG is a membership organization for independent publishers.

Publishers Association (PA)
www.publishers.org.uk
The Publishers Association is the leading trade organization serving book, journal, audio, and electronic publishers in the UK.

Society of Authors
www.societyofauthors.org
The Society is a membership organization with over 9,000 members writing in all areas of the profession. Authors are eligible to join after being offered a contract from a publisher, broadcaster or agent.

International

Association of Learned and Professional Society Publishers (ALPSP)
www.alpsp.org
With more than 340 member organizations in forty-one countries, ALPSP is the largest international trade association for scholarly and professional publishers.

EDItEUR
www.editeur.org
EDItEUR is the international group coordinating development of the standards infrastructure for electronic commerce in the book, e-book and serials sectors. EDItEUR administers the ONIX family of standards and provides management services for the International ISBN Agency.

GS1
www.gs1.org
GS1 is an international not-for-profit association with Member Organizations in more than 100 countries. GS1 is dedicated to the design and implementation of global standards and solutions to improve the efficiency and visibility of supply and demand chains globally and across sectors. The GS1 system of standards is the most widely used supply chain standards system in the world.

International Association of Scientific, Technical & Medical Publishers (STM)
www.stm-assoc.org
STM is the leading global trade association for academic and professional publishers. It has over 120 members in 21 countries who each year collectively publish nearly 66% of all journal articles and tens of thousands of monographs and reference works. STM members include learned societies, university presses, private companies, new starts and established players.

International ISBN Agency
www.isbn-international.org
The International ISBN Agency is the registration authority for the ISBN system.

International Organization for Standardization (ISO)

www.iso.org

ISO is the world's largest developer of voluntary International Standards. International Standards give state of the art specifications for products, services and good practice, helping to make industry more efficient and effective. Developed through global consensus, they help to break down barriers to international trade.

International Publishers Association (IPA)

www.internationalpublishers.org

The International Publishers Association (IPA) is an international industry federation representing all aspects of book and journal publishing. Established in 1896, IPA's mission is to promote and protect publishing and to raise awareness for publishing as a force for economic, cultural and political development. Around the world IPA actively fights against censorship and promotes copyright, literacy and freedom to publish. IPA is an industry association with a human rights mandate.

PEN International

www.pen-international.org

PEN International celebrates literature and promotes freedom of expression. Founded in 1921, the global community of writers now numbers more than 20,000 and spans more than 100 countries.

World Wide Web Consortium (W3C)

www.w3.org

W3C is an international community working to develop web standards. Led by Tim Berners-Lee, the W3C mission is the development of protocols and standards that ensure the long-term growth of the Web.

Vendor Directory

This Directory is not a comprehensive listing or an endorsement of vendors in the selected categories. It is intended as an overview of major companies whose services are related to topics discussed in The Metadata Handbook.

Book Data Aggregators/Book Data Licensing

BDS (Bibliographic Data Services)
www.bibliographicdata.co.uk

BDS offers data on books and home entertainment releases, web development and maintenance services, web-based applications on media to retailers, e-tailers, publishers, libraries, charities and government bodies.

R.R. Bowker
www.bowker.com

Bowker is a leading provider of bibliographic information and management solutions designed to help publishers, booksellers, and libraries better serve their customers. Bowker, an affiliated business of ProQuest and the official ISBN Agency for Australia, United States and U.S. territories, is headquartered in New Providence, New Jersey with additional operations in England and Australia.

Ingram Data Services
www.ingrambook.com/publishers

Ingram Data Services (IDS) manages one of the largest and most comprehensive databases in the industry. content@ingram® allows customers to receive title information directly from Ingram's comprehensive database to use in their own systems. Ingram's data includes detailed bibliographic information and metadata.

Nielsen BookData
www.nielsenbookdata.co.uk

Nielsen BookData Information service provides data services to more than 100 countries worldwide. Nielsen collects book information from over 70 countries (including the UK, Ireland, Europe, Australia, New Zealand and South Africa) and works closely with the leading data providers in the U.S. Nielsen also administers the ISBN Registry service for the UK and Ireland.

Wholesalers

Baker & Taylor
www.btol.com

In business since 1828, Baker & Taylor supplies books, multimedia, and related information services to U.S. retailers and libraries. Baker & Taylor maintains about 385,000 titles in inventory with more than 1.5 million titles available for order. They offer a full range of library services, including cataloging and collection development.

YBP Library Services
www.ybp.com

YBP is a Baker & Taylor company specializing in materials and services for the academic library market.

Bertrams

www.bertrams.com

Bertrams is a leading UK book wholesaler, library supplier, and publisher distribution service.

Brodart

www.brodartbooks.com

Brodart specializes in library services, providing materials, cataloging, physical processing, and collection development.

Follett

www.follett.com

Follett is a wholesaler of educational materials, college textbooks, collegiate merchandise, and course administration. Divisions include Follett Higher Education, Follett Library Resources, and Follett Educational Services.

Gardners Books

www.gardners.com

Gardners is a major British wholesaler, providing materials mainly to retail outlets.

Ingram Book Company

www.ingrambook.com

Ingram Book Company, an Ingram Content Group company, is the largest book wholesale distributor in the world, offering immediate access to more than two million titles. Ingram is a provider for more than 71,000 retail and library customers globally. Ingram Library Services offers value-added services such as cataloging and collection development.

Raincoast Book Distribution, Inc.

www.raincoast.com

Raincoast Book Distribution is an award winning, Canadian-owned book wholesale and distribution company based in Vancouver, BC. Divisions include Raincoast Books and Publishers Group Canada distribution companies.

Distributors

Bertram Publisher Services

www.bertrams.com

Bertram Publisher Services (BPS) provides distribution solutions for a range of publishing and book industry clients.

GBS (Grantham Book Services)

www.granthambookservices.co.uk

GBS is a leading UK distributor for independent publishers.

Independent Publishers Group

www.ipgbook.com

Independent Publishers Group was founded in 1971, the first organization specifically created for the purpose of representing titles from independent presses to the book trade.

Ingram Publisher Services

www.ingrampublisherservices.com

Ingram Publisher Services Inc. is a full-service distributor for publishers of all sizes, currently representing more than 60 clients from around the world.

Publishers Group Canada

www.pgcbooks.ca

A division of Raincoast Book Distribution, Inc., PGC Books offers full-service Canadian distribution to over 150 independent and specialty publishing houses worldwide.

Publishers Group UK

www.pguk.co.uk

Publishers Group UK (PGUK) offers sales, marketing and fulfillment services to publishers primarily from the USA and the UK.

Raincoast Books
www.raincoast.com
Raincoast Books is a full-service Canadian distribution company.

TBS (The Book Service)
www.thebookservice.co.uk
TBS is a leading UK book distributor with over 100 million books distributed annually.

Ebook Aggregators

Canadian Electronic Library
www.canadianelectroniclibrary.ca
Canadian Electronic Library is an aggregator of books from Canadian publishers for libraries.

Dawsonera – Dawson Books
www.dawsonera.com
Dawsonera is a web-based collection of ebooks designed for use in libraries.

ebrary – Proquest
www.ebrary.com
ebrary currently has more than 4,500 library customers around the world serving more than 19.2 million end-users. More than 500 of the world's most authoritative publishers distribute e-books on the ebrary platform.

Ebook Library - Proquest
www.eblib.com
EBL provides ebooks to academic and research, government and corporate libraries, specifically in the areas of science, technology, and medicine.

EBSCO ebooks
www.ebscohost.com/ebooks
EBSCO offers hundreds of thousands of ebook and audiobook titles from leading publishers via ebooks on EBSCOHost.

Gibson Library Connections
www.gibsonlibraryconnections.ca
Gibson Library Connections is a sales agency presenting international publishers to the Canadian library market. Products offered include databases, digital collections and e-books.

OverDrive
www.overdrive.com
OverDrive is a full-service digital distributor of ebooks, audiobooks, and other digital content. OverDrive delivers secure management, DRM protection, and download fulfillment services for publishers, libraries, schools, and retailers.

MyiLibrary® – Ingram Content Group
www.myilibrary.com
MyiLibrary® is an industry-leading e-content aggregation platform for public, academic and professional libraries around the world.

Business, Content, and Metadata Management Vendors

Avatar
www.avatar-software.com
AVATAR is a fully integrated, module based business management system, specifically designed to meet the evolving needs of publishers and distributors. It has been developed and is supported by Littlejohn, one of the UK's top 30 firms of chartered accountants, based in London. In addition to its core financial management ledgers, AVATAR modules include Title Management, Rights and Royalties and Business Intelligence. The AVATAR system is ONIX compliant.

Cyberwolf
www.cyberwolf.com

ACUMEN Book™ : ACUMEN Book™ is an integrated business management system built on a client-server architecture. It is suitable for sites with up to 100 concurrent users. The Product Marketing component allows information export in a customizable format for transmission to trading partners and publisher websites.

IBS BookMaster
www.ibs.net/products/ibs-media/bookmaster

BookMaster is a publishing-specific integrated Enterprise Management business software solution for publishers and book distributors, print and digital. Comprised of core distribution, financial and Supply Chain Management (SCM) system with highly functional integration to web-based financial transaction and business management processes.

Klopotek
www.klopotek.de

Product Planning and Management (PPM) Products:

- **Title Management and Product Marketing:** Facilitates ONIX creation and distribution to multiple trading partners.
- **Editorial and Production:** Tools for management of title planning and production activities and workflows.
- **Contracts, Rights, & Royalties:** Tools for contract, royalty, and rights management. Royalty reporting matches EDItEUR and BISG requirements.

Firebrand Technologies
www.firebrandtech.com

- **Title Management Solutions:** Facilitates tracking titles from pre-acquisition through post-production.
- **Eloquence Metadata Solutions:** Provides ONIX implementation and metadata distribution services.
- **Ecommerce Solutions:** Pre-developed website architecture integrated with Firebrand's Title Management Solutions.

NetRead
www.netread.com

Jacketcaster: Offers conversion to ONIX for Books and metadata distribution services with file formatting per trading partner specifications.

ONIXEDIT
www.onixedit.com

ONIXEDIT title management software is based on the ONIX standard. Functionality includes the ability to read and write ONIX, export and transmit ONIX, validate and save files in specific formats.

Onixsuite
www.onixsuite.com

Onixsuite is a cloud-based system that allows publishers, retailers, authors, and distributors to easily create, correct, enhance, display and distribute their book metadata, with no proficiency in ONIX required. It is available in multiple languages.

Publishing Technology
www.publishingtechnology.com

Advance™ Product Manager: Management of product information, production processes and schedules, digital assets. Allows import, export, and distribution of data in various formats, including ONIX.

Scott Moore Ltd.
www.scottmoore.co.uk

Book Manager: Incorporates a range of business functions including catalog production and direct marketing, royalties, and electronic data exchange. Book Manager has a module that can import, export and manage ONIX for Books data.

Stison Publishing Solutions
www.stison.com

- **Title Manager:** A web-based bibliographic data storage, management, and distribution system that is ONIX compliant.

- **Production Manager:** A production scheduling, reporting, and workflow management system. Other Stison modules include **Royalty Manager**, **Web Manager**, and **e-book manager**.

Virtusales
www.virtusales.com

- **Biblio3:** An integrated, modular publishing management system. Functionality includes production management, rights and royalties management, bibliographic and editorial data management. Data management components include centralized storage, XML output for catalog creation, and ONIX Wizard and feed generator.

- **BiblioDAM:** A digital asset management system. When integrated with Biblo3, metadata from Biblio3 automatically feeds in the BiblioDAM system.

- **BiblioLIVE:** An online version of Biblio tools that includes backups and disaster recovery.

Ebook Production, Conversion, Digitization, Distribution, & Print-On-Demand

Business-to-Business Services

Aptara
www.aptaracorp.com
Digital media production for multiple platforms including e-readers, smart phones, table, PC, and Web.

Exemplarr
www.exemplarr.com
Conversion, production, and printing services.

Book Masters
www.bookmasters.com/publishers
Production, print-on-demand, conversion, and ebook distribution services for publishers.

CodeMantra
www.codemantra.com
Production and conversion services.

CoreSource® – Ingram
www.ingramcontent.com
Digital asset management services and ebook distribution to more than 160 partners.

DeMarque
www.demarque.com
Ebook distribution services, mainly for French-language books in the Canadian market.

eBOUND Canada
www.eboundcanada.org
Provides digital asset management, ebook conversion, and retail distribution services for Association of Canadian Publishers members. Partners with Ingram's CoreSource® for DAM services and with Follett of Canada to offer eBOUND resources to students.

ePubDirect
www.epubdirect.com
Provides storage and ebook distribution to retailers and libraries along with billing, administrative, and business intelligence services.

Espresso Book Machine®
www.ondemandbooks.com
On-site print-on-demand for retail bookstores, college stores, and libraries. Connects to Google

Books, Lightning Source, Open Content Alliance, and others through **EspressNet** software.

Firebrand Technologies
www.firebrandtech.com
Quality File Conversion through partnerships with eBook Architects, led by industry-acknowledged eBook formatting expert Joshua Tallent, and Digital Divide Data.

PubFactory
www.pubfactory.net
PubFactory is an online publishing application for books, reference works, and journals in a variety of XML formats, with full support for PDF, images and other rich media.

Impelys
www.impelsys.com

- **iPublish Central**
  www.impelsys.com/ipublishcentral
  iPublishCentral is a comprehensive platform that allows publishers to warehouse, deliver, distribute, market and sell their eBooks. Other iPublish products include iPublish Custom, iPublish Central Mobile Apps, and Publisher Marketing Tools.

Innodata
www.innodata.com/services/epublishing
Ebook production, conversion, and distribution.

Jouve
www.jouve.com
Conversion services.

LibreDigital – RR Donnelly
www.rrdonnelley.com/libredigital
Content conversion, content management, and delivery services for books and magazines. Also offer an HTML5 browser-based reader that can be integrated into web sites.

Lightning Source - Ingram
www.lightningsource.com
Print-on-demand and distribution through print-to-order (distribution partners place orders) and print-to-publisher (publishers place orders) services.

Ninestars
www.ninestars.in
Digitization and conversion services.

Contentra Technologies
www.contentratechnologies.com
Production and conversion services.

Reality Premedia Services
www.realitypremedia.com
Ebook conversion, production, and print-on-demand services.

Self-Publishing Services

Author Solutions
www.authorsolutions.com
Recently acquired by Penquin, Author Solutions offers self-publishing services for print and digital under several brands including **Author House, Book Tango, Trafford, and iUniverse.**

BookBaby
www.bookbaby.com
BookBaby provides ebook production, conversion, and distribution services for self-published authors. They also offer print-on-demand services.

Book Masters
www.bookmasters.com/author
Book Masters offers print and ebook production packages for self-publishers.

CreateSpace/Amazon
www.createspace.com
Amazon's print production and print-on-demand services sold on Amazon sites with expanded distribution to other sellers for an additional fee. CreateSpace-assigned ISBNs can only be used with the CreateSpace Independent Publishing Platform but ISBN information can be registered with booksinprint.com.

Lulu
www.lulu.com
Ebook production, conversion, print-on-demand, and distribution services for self-published authors. Maintains Lulu Marketplace online store and distributes ebook and print to iBookstore, Barnes & Noble, and others.

Self-Publishing, Inc.
www.selfpublishing.com
Production and print-on-demand services.

Smashwords
www.smashwords.com
Smashwords provides production and distribution of self-published and indie ebooks. Maintains an online store and distributes to iBookstore, Barnes & Noble, and others.

Ebook Self-Publishing Services for Proprietary Reading Devices

Kindle Direct Publishing/Amazon
www.kdp.amazon.com
Authors can start the production process through Kindle Direct or convert an existing publication with one of Kindle's partners (Aptara, CodeMantra, etc.). Print books already published through CreateSpace can be converted through CreateSpace. Kindle ebooks are only sold on Amazon sites. Distribution through other partners will require different ebook formats and a relationship with another selling partner or with an ebook distributor that works with multiple vendors. Amazon does not require an ISBN. Amazon-assigned identifiers are not valid outside Amazon selling platforms and other vendors may require a valid ISBN. Metadata is entered through the Kindle Direct interface and does not allow (or require) all of the data elements available to publishers using ONIX or other metadata distribution methods and formats.

Kobo Writing Life
www.kobobooks.com/kobowritinglife
The Kobo Writing Life conversion process converts files to the EPUB format. Kobo ebooks are not limited to distribution through the Kobo ebook store. The self-publisher is free to distribute and sell elsewhere and Kobo has partnerships with Chapters/Indigo (Canada), W.H. Smith (UK), as well as vendors in France and Australia. Kobo requires a valid ISBN and requires metadata submission in ONIX or Excel format.

NOOK Press
nookpress.com
Nook Press is an online, self-service web portal for uploading ebooks for sale on the Barnes and Noble eBookstore. Nook Press does not require an ISBN. Nook Press-assigned identifiers are not valid outside Barnes & Noble selling platforms and other vendors may require a valid ISBN. Metadata is entered through the Nook Press interface and does not allow (or require) all of the data elements available to publishers using ONIX or other metadata distribution methods and formats.

About the Authors

Renée Register
www.datacurate.com

Renée Register is also author of the *DataCurate Quick Guide* series, including The Essential Guide to Metadata for Books, Metadata Best Practices and Industry Certification, and Optimizing Metadata for Digital Publishing. She developed and instructs a series of classes on metadata for Digital Book World University and conducts webinars and workshops on book metadata.

She specializes in the development of metadata management practices to optimize content discovery, internal operations, and business intelligence. Her company, DataCurate, is focused on products and services to help publishing professionals meet the information demands of the 21st century marketplace.

Renée has over 20 years' experience in building and growing innovative metadata systems, products, and services for materials vendors, metadata providers, and libraries. She holds a master's degree in Library and Information Science and her experience includes ten years with Ingram Book Group and six years with OCLC, a non-profit library cooperative.

Renée Register's profile on LinkedIn.

You can reach Renée at:
reneeregister@datacurate.com

Thad McIlroy
www.thefutureofpublishing.com

Thad McIlroy is an electronic publishing analyst and author based in San Francisco and Vancouver.

His site, www.thefutureofpublishing.com, is the most thorough exploration of where publishing is headed. McIlroy provides consulting services to publishing and media companies, design and advertising agencies, as well as the full range of vendors serving the publishing industry. Having authored a dozen books and over 300 articles on these subjects, he serves also as an expert witness on patent litigation in the media industries. McIlroy served also for five years as Program Director for Seybold Seminars.

McIlroy is a contributing writer to *PrintAction* magazine and on the editorial board of the journal *Learned Publishing* and the Canadian literary journal, *Geist*. He is a member of the Association for Computing Machinery (ACM), the Electronic Frontier Foundation (EFF), and the Technical Association of the Graphic Arts (TAGA). He co-authored both the first and the second editions of *The Metadata Handbook*. His latest book is *Mobile Strategies for Digital Publishing: A Practical Guide to the Evolving Landscape.*

During the past 25 years he has educated and entertained audiences around the world on every aspect of digital and print publishing including the Intelligent Content Conference, Gilbane Content Management, the Henry Stewart DAM conference, XPLOR, Seybold Conferences, ePublishing (Denmark), the I S & T Annual Conference, and Prepress Asia.

Thad McIlroy's profile on LinkedIn.

You can reach Thad at:
thad@thefutureofpublishing.com

About the Designer

Adam Rowe
www.admrwe.com

The layout and graphic design for *The Metadata Handbook* are by Adam Rowe. Adam is a graphic designer based out of Chicago. He received his degree from the College for Creative Studies in Detroit and specializes in identity and information design. Adam also created the graphic design and logo for the DataCurate site.